NOT UNCOMMON, Just Unheard Of

A memoir by esther morris leidolf
From union carpenter to gender activist

Edited by Susan K. Jacoby

Design by Jacob R. Leidolf
Cover Artwork by ANKANA
Cover inspired by the Intersex flag, designed by Morgan Carpenter,
Australia, 2013

This memoir is a composite of multiple work and rehab experiences. Most names have been changed or removed when possible, including mine. I chose the name Jean, to create some distance between me and the events in this book. Life is a process.

I decided to ignore the sound advice to pursue traditional editing and publishing. I had very little choice with the experiences that became this book so I needed to control the way that I tell them. That said, I want to thank my readers: Ann, Ani, Jacky, Jake, Libby and Pat. I appreciate your support, your feedback and your respect for my words more than I can say. I did however rely on Susan as chief editor. Your friendship and tenderness with my words kept me going. I couldn't have finished this book without you.

ISBN: 979-8-9879952-1-1
Library of Congress Control Number: 2023907033
Copyright 2023

For my sister Libby, who gave me what I needed before I knew I needed it.

TABLE OF CONTENTS

New Day, A New Job

So. This is it, I thought as I carried my tools through the loading dock to the coffee truck. I paid for a light coffee and turned to face the crowd. Workers of different trades were scattered in their separate little clusters waiting for the seven A.M. whistle. From this view I understood the comradery that came from sharing the danger, and the disrespect of working in the trades. Watching them interact with each other gave me a sense of who might have my back and who might want to break it. I wandered through the loading dock, coffee in one hand and tool box in the other, awed by the size of the job. The building boom of the 80's brought a lot of work to the city and this was the best job in town. I knew I was there to satisfy multiple quotas for federal subsidies. I was a female, a city resident and an apprentice. Three quotas in one hire, but at the end of the day I knew they didn't want me there. I wasn't as threatened as I might have been since I never really felt I belonged anywhere.

"You must be the new broaaaa, um girl for Unlimited."

I turned to the craggy voice behind me. "Yea." I tried not to show any expression. I wasn't sure what to express so I kept it simple. "I'm Jean."

"I'm Smitty, the carpenter steward. I can always spot the new girls on the job. You can leave your tools in there." He pointed to a trailer. "And bring your coffee. I'll get you all signed up."

"Thanks," I replied. I stepped in and slid my toolbox under the lunch table near the others, wondering if it would

1

be there when I got back. Or even worse, what would be added to it? I have found dead rodents, human excrement and ketchup covered tampons tossed in with my tools more than once. The fascination men on construction sites have with menstruation is just plain bizarre, and always made me uncomfortable. I walked with Smitty through the loading dock and down a flight of stairs. We wound our way through a maze of corridors to the shack for Unlimited. Each company has their own plywood shack to serve as an on-site office where workers gather in the morning for their orders and supplies.

"Morning Ed. This is Jean, the new girl. She's all yours now. Good luck!" Smitty left with a sidelong glance toward me and Ed.

Ed looked at me as though there was nothing to say and started for the door. "This way, honey. Done much rockin'? You still an apprentice? Where'd you work last? Who for? What are you doing in this racket anyway? You should be a finish-man, not hanging sheetrock."

We backtracked our way to the loading dock. When Ed finally took a breath, I replied. "I'm a fourth year apprentice. I worked for ten months on the hospital job site, framing mostly. I hung a little board there too. I have residential sheetrock experience, but nothing like this. I did do a lot of finish work when I ran my own business though."

"I can promise you an experience here like no other!" Ed chuckled.

I wondered if he meant the work or the workers but I tried not to think about it.

"For now you'll be working on Louis's crew in the office tower," he explained as we returned to the loading dock.

"Who's the broad?"

Ed turned. "Morning, Louis. She's a female not a broad. We don't have broads no more."

Females? They spoke about me as though I was a specimen to observe. I felt like a new toy. I have had that feeling before and I didn't like it. My spirits picked up when I returned to find my tools were as I left them.

"Take her up to work with the Wood brothers on the tenth floor," Ed said. He walked off without another word.

Louis led the way to the elevator. He walked swiftly. The hammer-hoop on his belt squeaked with every other step. He swung his arms awkwardly. He said nothing until we reached the elevator. "Ten, Freddy."

"This your new girl?" Freddy asked.

I took a breath and exhaled slowly, thinking, *Oh great. They think he owns me now.*

"Kinda skinny for hangin' board aren't ya honey?" Freddy asked as we started to ascend.

"I'll be framing with the Wood brothers for now I guess." Louis added the first of many unsolicited opinions. "I hear she's kinda smart. Metal studs shouldn't be too much for her."

"Here's ten. Good luck toots." Freddy opened the gates of the elevator cage.

"Thanks Freddy." I said, and turned to face him. "My name's Jean by the way. I'll see you around." I learned early on to make eye contact as soon as possible. It seems to help the good guys see me as a person, not another broad trying to steal their jobs. As for the not so good guys-I saw that in their eyes too.

Louis and I entered the office tower section of the complex as the elevator gates banged shut behind us.

"You'll be framing with the Wood brothers," Louis explained as he put an arm around my shoulders.

"Is that so?" I smiled and stepped out of reach.

"Whooa, no offense honey. I'm the kinda guy who talk with his hands is all. I'm not trying to get familiar."

"Well I'm a Quaker and I prefer silence if you don't mind."

Louis gave me a questioning look, then yelled over to the two men standing by a large rectangular metal box with a hinged top. "Hey Kevin, Teddy, I got a new recruit for yas!"

They turned. Kevin was a chubby short man in his mid-forties, slightly balding with a cheery smile that felt welcoming. Teddy, taller and younger than his brother, had a full head of bushy hair that really needed a comb.

"Nice to meet you," Kevin said as he offered a hand. "It's always nice to have a sweet face around in a dump like this."

"Catching up on your quotas again, Louis?" Teddy asked with a smile as he reached out to shake my hand.

"Ahhh shut up, wise guy. Two broads in a hundred is plenty enough for me!" Louis reached into the gang box where we were all standing and pulled out a hard hat. "This is a hard hat job, honey. You gotta wear it at all times." Then he was gone.

I glanced around the building. No one else was on the floor. The outside walls of the building were concrete and glass. One section of glass had been removed so supplies could be delivered by crane from outside. The air was stale. I could see dust particles and god knows what else glimmer in the sunlight. The place felt like a vast emptiness, broken slightly by pallets of metal studs and sheetrock. There were no interior walls, just an open space in the center from top to bottom.

"That's the atrium." Kevin said. "We won't be working there. We're the light pocket crew. Ever install light pockets, Jean?"

I shook my head *no* as we put on our tool belts. Teddy walked off to the other side of the atrium with his tool bucket, an extension cord and a screw gun.

"Teddy likes to work alone. Don't be offended, he always does. Been that way since 'Nam. We'll be partners, if you don't mind." Kevin spoke quietly.

"Fine by me." I replied and filled my tool belt with hand tools and screws from the gang box. "What's the procedure here?"

"Well..." Kevin started again. "Most of the ceilings here are suspended tile. That's not our job. We've got to create the light pockets... So what we gotta do is make soffits- you know... a space in the ceiling for the light fixtures that will hide all the electrical wiring. But first things first." Kevin reached into the gang box and pulled out a radio. Tuning in a 1950's station he started dancing and bopping to the music.

I was really shocked by his silliness and found it refreshing compared to experiences I'd had with other partners.

Together we gathered extension cords and screw guns to take to the staging where Kevin had worked the day before. I looked up at the metal studs hanging from the ceiling, and vaguely pictured what our work entailed.

"What are you comfortable with, sister?" Kevin asked.

I could not believe that he asked and appreciated the way he spoke to me, not at me. "I'm a pretty good cutter. I usually work in some kind of mill," I paused. "And, umm, well I don't do well with heights. "I glanced over to the center of the building to the thirty-eight stories of staging from the ground floor to the skylight in the atrium.

"Fine," Kevin said simply. "I'll measure and you cut. Don't worry. There's this unofficial rule about women on the center staging anyway. Most of our work is right here along the edge. You are gonna have to work off this rolling staging with me though. Besides, it's no taller than you are." We both laughed.

"No problem there." I replied as I approached.

Kevin motioned for me to join him on the staging platform. The staging was six feet high, three feet wide, and five feet long. The wheels locked to prevent it from moving. I climbed up the side and onto the platform next to Kevin.

He went on with the details of the job. "See that mark over there on that steel column? That's our elevation, or the grade-mark for the soffit height." He turned and pointed in the other direction. "And there's a mark on the column over there." I nodded and looked as he pointed to another steel column thirty feet away. "Our job is to connect the dots, so to speak." Kevin spoke in pauses. I could feel him watch me as he spoke. A silent bond was being established as we sized each other up. He continued in a matter of fact tone. "Then we have to frame it, so we can close it up with sheetrock and just like that; bing-bam-boom, we have light pockets. Feel free to ask questions. We're a team, ya know. You'll catch on. Let's just get started and you'll see how it all comes together. You mind getting down to get two bundles of track, and a bundle of studs? You can use the pallet of sheetrock as a workbench. I need you to roll me over to that column so I can pull my dry-line across." Kevin pointed to the column in the far corner. He had already tied one end of his dry-line around

6

the column near the first grade-mark. I unlocked the wheels of the staging with the toe of my work boot. Kevin unraveled his spool of dry-line above us as I rolled the staging toward the other column. When we reached the other side, he tied the dry-line around the column which then connected the dots. I locked the wheels and climbed back up to join him.

"Now that we have the line on each grade-mark we can measure the stud length from the decking above, to the dry-line here." Again, he pointed to the different areas as he referred to them. "Yesterday I laid-out the top track, and screwed it to the decking there." As he pointed, I could see where he had screwed the top track to the metal decking of the ceiling above. "Now you can cut studs...Ready?"

I climbed back down and asked. "What's your length?"

"Twenty-six and three quarters." Kevin watched me hook the tape measure over the end and pull it along the inside of the hollow metal stud. I snipped the stud to mark the length, dropped my tape measure into my tool pouch and cut the stud to length. When I handed him the piece, he checked my accuracy as I knew he would.

"Nothing personal," he said. "But I'm responsible if we blow it."

"Not to worry," I replied as I cut more studs.

"What time is it getting to be?" He asked.

"Ten past nine. When's coffee around here? Nobody said anything to me about getting the coffee order." As a fourth year apprentice I knew I had rank over younger apprentices but women were still assigned coffee duty regardless of our seniority. Choosing your battles over stupid stuff eventually beats you down, but you also have to draw the line from the start to show them how much crap you will take. It's a tough line to balance and changes with every job. Sometimes getting coffee was a welcome break from your partner, or a good excuse to take a walk. Other times it was used to show status.

"Relax. You're only responsible for the floor you're working on. Teddy and I bring our own. The truck comes at nine fifteen, so you better get going if you want something for yourself."

I headed back to the loading dock to get my coffee. I was feeling good about my work so far, and about Kevin too. As I got my coffee, I heard a woman's voice amidst the throng of hungry men.

I turned and saw Ruth, a plumber's apprentice I knew from another job. "Hey, nice to see YOU here! Have you been on this job long?"

"Not as long as this coffee has!" Ruth said, and then answered. "I started last month."

"This is my first day. God, this job is enormous. I think I lucked out with my partner though."

"Who are you working with?" Ruth asked as she made coffee, tea, and sandwiches for her crew.

"The Wood brothers, Kevin mostly."

"Oh yea. I met them at the elevator. They're pretty nice guys. They've got to be better than the asshole I got stuck with!" Ruth moaned. "He keeps touching my hands, and making really nasty jokes about the female end and the male end of the pipe fittings."

"I'm sorry, Ruth. If he's harassing you that bad, maybe you should talk to your steward. Maybe you can switch partners."

"He IS my STEWARD!" she moaned even louder. "And a real son-of-a-bitch!"

"Oh shit. You do have a problem." I knew how it felt when your steward didn't have your back.

"Well I should go. Let's have lunch in the park across the street." Ruth disappeared around the corner.

I went back to the tenth floor to have my coffee with Kevin and Teddy. Fifteen minutes later, Teddy went back to his side of the atrium and Kevin and I resumed our roles. Kevin measured stud lengths from the staging, and I cut them from my workstation of sheetrock on the floor. He laid out the spacing on the track where the studs would be attached. I kept cutting, and he kept checking my accuracy; an insult I had to ignore. I kept up with his pace, and cut each stud exactly as he requested. It got a bit boring after a while. Mark the stud, bend it over and cut it off... Mark the stud, bend it over and cut it off. The radio broke the monotony and we both sang along.

I could hear power saws cutting through different materials and wondered which trades might be working nearby from the sounds. Power tools make a specific sound depending on what they're cutting, making construction jobs sound like an industrial jazz ensemble. I could hear the tin-knockers cutting metal ductwork, plumbers drilling through concrete and carpenters cutting wood. Someone needed a new blade.

By the end of the day Kevin stopped checking my work and I relaxed a little. I couldn't help but wonder if he would have been so prudent checking the work of a male apprentice; but nonetheless we shared a comfortable rhythm throughout the day.

I got to work early the next morning. I always tried to play the game right without being sucked into the culture of the game. It is a drain balancing the line between the role I needed to play to survive and my reaction to that role. I wanted it so I played along. I wanted to finish my apprenticeship, get my credential and get the hell out. I only had a few months left and I was determined to finish before being beaten by it. There was limited support out there and I was determined to make it stronger by my own survival.

I walked through the loading dock towards the elevator, taking my time to ease the transition between my life at home and the different world of work. I saw Ruth and remembered I was not alone.

The brothers greeted me in unison at the elevator.

"Lovely summer day," I replied. "How are you guys doing this morning?"

"We're here aren't we?" Teddy mumbled in a sleepy tone.

Freddy appeared at seven sharp. "Going up," he announced.

A group of workers piled in. The first load was too crowded so the three of us waited for Freddy's return. The crowd of workers waiting for the elevator got larger so we had to squeeze on for the second trip. Before we started moving, there were all kinds of grunts and hooting sounds made at my expense. The guy behind me was standing much closer than he needed to and asked, "Hey honey, if I tell you that you have a great body will you hold it against me?" My face got hotter as they all laughed. I closed my eyes and tried to ride it out to the tenth floor. Five. Six. Seven.

"Sure would like to get into her pants," someone else said, followed by more hoots and laughter. No one pushed back. Even my partners let that slide. I turned to face the crowd as the elevator gates clanged open on our floor. "Sorry sport, but I don't need another asshole in my pants." Teddy and Kevin just stared at me as I walked past them onto the floor. I was livid and scared and well aware that showing it would work against me.

We shared a cautious silence as we walked over to the gang box to start our day. I was still furious, but calming down. Second day on the job and my defenses were on overdrive for reasons unrelated to work. The power men have to victimize women strips away an additional layer of safety for women in male dominated careers.

"Good one Jean," Teddy said finally. "A sting like that will be all over the job by morning coffee."

Kevin added, "Second day on the job and they're already talking 'bout ya. You stopped him good though," Kevin grinned.

I knew they were trying to make me believe I'd won a small battle, but it didn't feel that way. I smiled and nodded to acknowledge their efforts. It wasn't my job to make them feel supportive after the fact when they could have stepped in when it happened.

We put on our tool belts, filled them with supplies and set off for our work areas. I couldn't shed my resentment and I struggled to keep up with Kevin's jolly mood. Sensing my mood, he kept it up until he was able to bring me out of it. I knew and liked what he was trying to do, but I couldn't put the burden aside.

Work partners are significant others of sorts. You have to trust them with your life and navigate personalities for at least eight hours a day. If you're lucky enough to get a good one, you relish it while it lasts. But you dare not get hooked because they don't last long. Every job ends and people move on. You have to work with what you've got and make the best of it. We worked in silence through the morning until Kevin finally said, "Look Jean, some of these guys are just plain jerks. Don't take it personally."

I have always hated that command. "But I am a person so how else should I take it? Do they act like that when it's just you boys on board?"

"No," he answered quietly. "You've got a point there..."

"Damn straight. I just want to do my job and get paid like everybody else."

"But you're not like everybody else." Kevin chuckled and added, "I'm glad too."

His kind remark made me smile. "I know it's hard for some of these guys to accept women on the job site. But it's more basic than that. There is something about this ridiculous need that some men have to destroy anything they can't seduce or understand... and the audacity to assume that they get to understand something before they can accept it... like the world is waiting to be blessed by their approval..." I stared across the floor and gazed at the dust particles floating in the sunlight. "I don't expect open arms here. And I have no intention of invading this boys club either. So what's the big deal anyway? I just want to earn a living doing the work I like to do."

"For what it's worth, Jean, it doesn't matter who you are. It's just the fact that you're here."

"Oh thanks, Kevin. That's just pisser. I feel much better knowing I don't have a personality problem, just a personality." We both laughed at the absurdity.

Kevin was taking measurements and repeating them to me. "Well, I never thought much about it; but it doesn't matter to me either. You have to remember that you ARE an undesirable here. It takes some getting used to, too. Some people will always resist change. I don't understand why you want to be where you're not wanted. But as long as you can keep up I don't care."

Kevin signaled for me to join him on the staging platform. "Fill up with screws and bring up a bundle of track, will ya? Oh, and tie the extension cord to the staging so it won't get unplugged while we're up here."

Happy to leave the conversation behind I passed Kevin the stock, then tied the cord around the frame of our staging and climbed up to join him.

He had already screwed the top track onto the ceiling and attached the studs I had cut earlier. They were hanging loose in the air like a picket fence without a bottom rail. "Now we're gonna screw on the bottom track. First, we have to reinforce the bottom track with plywood, to hold the weight of the light pockets. Then we brace it to the decking above to make it straight all-way-round. You know, plumb it up. How about you hop down and rip the strips of plywood?" Once we got our supplies set up it was time to break for lunch.

I walked across the street to the park to join Ruth, who was sitting under a tree with a few other women from the site. We chatted while we ate our lunches, and I felt reassured by meeting other women on the job. All eyes were on us as the five of us walked through the loading dock after lunch. Shocked that we posed such a threat to this environment, we went our separate ways.

The next morning Smitty was waiting by the elevator. "I hope you don't mind working weekends. There's a lot of overtime coming up. You could make real good money on this job if you stick around. How are things going so far?"

"Not bad," I told him.

"Good then. You getting along with the brothers all right? They're good men those two. Good mechanics too. It's a shame they're not from our local. The ratio of company-men from outta state is getting outta hand. I'm sorry to say that when the time comes they will be the first to go. Real gentlemen, those boys. I arranged for you to work with them ya know. "

Yeah right! I thought and nodded, "Thanks Smitty. I've been working with Kevin mostly."

"Enjoy it while it lasts," Smitty said as he trotted off.

We shared our usual greeting as we loaded our tool belts and talked about the day ahead of us. Fridays are slower days, meant for tying up the loose ends of the weeks' work. On his side, Teddy was laying-out the top track for the soffits. Kevin and I finished framing and were preparing to reinforce the metal track on the bottom with plywood as we had done the day before.

Louis appeared out of nowhere. His hammer hoop squeaked as he walked over to speak to Kevin.

"Don't tell me about it. Tell her. She's not deaf yet, ya know," Kevin snapped. Actually, my hearing has always been a problem but that had been dismissed as lack of attention.

Oh shit, news does travel fast around here, I thought as I prepared myself for a lecture about talking back to the jerk in the elevator.

Louis sauntered over to where I was working. "I don't want to see you using the power saw," he said to my surprise. "You're just an apprentice."

"Wait. What?" I laughed. "Just an apprentice? Doesn't being an apprentice mean I am here to learn my trade? Or is it that I'm just a girl?" I quipped as I pulled the trigger to resume cutting.

"I don't want to see you hurt yourself," Louis said defensively. "It's my job. I'm your foreman. As an apprentice you have to be careful. I'm sure you heard about the carpenter apprentice who fell through the elevator shaft last week. Kid was in his early twenties. Nothing like that is going to happen on my job. I don't want you kids getting hurt."

I looked at the missing digits on Louis's left hand. "How am I to learn my trade if you don't want me doing anything? Don't use power tools? What the hell, man?" I wasn't yelling as much as I was shocked to be having this conversation.

Kevin stepped in. "Is there a problem, Louis?"

"Like I told ya; I don't like to see these girls doing any of the dangerous stuff."

"If you don't want to see her working then go away," Kevin laughed.

I added. "I'm supposed to watch while you work on the staging and jump down to do all the cutting too. Then Louis can come along and fire me for not doing anything. He'll tell everybody women in the trades can't keep up so he had to let me go! Isn't that the way it works Louis? You prevent us from doing our jobs and then fire us for not doing our jobs?" I continued cutting strips of plywood, glad the noise was drowning out the rest of what I had to say.

"Come on sister, forget about him. We have work to do." Kevin and I walked away leaving Louis standing alone with his hands in his pockets.

What Am I Doing Here?

Monday morning I got to the job early and struggled to push myself inside. The weekend had been such a different life. *I moved to the city for the women's community, and look at me now-the only woman in view.* I muttered to myself as I forced each step. What the hell am I doing here? It felt right in an intangible sort of way. Being the only one was a familiar feeling. I was the only girl a lot when I was a kid so that wasn't such a big deal. But this felt deeper than that. No matter where I was or who I was with I never felt a sense of belonging; more like a poser, inauthentic to my true self. I was so accustomed to feeling out of place that it actually felt normal to be off in the margins. Now I was in an occupation where I wasn't wanted at all. I couldn't think about it much but lingering questions were a constant companion. *Is working in physical labor my way of gaining a sense of physical integrity?* This was too much to think about and hardly the place to explore my emotions, my secrets, or my vulnerabilities. I had to keep all my reserves for my physical safety. I couldn't protect myself when I was a kid but I can protect myself now. I was relieved to look up to see the Wood brothers waiting at the elevator, which brought me back to the present.

"Good morning sister. Looks like you had a refreshing weekend for yourself."

"Sure enough. I went camping with some friends."

A man I had never seen before joined the conversation. "Did you go away with Ann?"

HUH? I turned toward this man who knew too much. My eyes followed him as he passed by. How in the world could he know enough to ask that when I didn't even know who he was? The stranger left as quickly as he appeared. I turned back to my partners. "Who was that?"

"He's one of us," Kevin explained.

"One of whom?" I queried, laughing.

"He used to be a foreman here for Unlimited, but they found a way to replace him with Louis. He's a wise-ass, but harmless."

Harmless? I didn't think so. He knew something about my private life. It's bad enough to be seen as a threat to employment but to be seen as a threat in their bedrooms was more than some men could bear. My mind was already clicking into survival mode and the workday had not yet begun.

"Going up." Freddy's call broke my train of thought. It was seven sharp.

After a quiet ride to our floor, we got off to start a new week. Louis, Ed and Burt met us at the gang box. The box was open. All the screw guns, cords and nail guns were gone. Everything that Unlimited had supplied us with had been stolen.

"Not again." Teddy moaned.

Burt was another new face to me. He had a self-important air about him. He was five foot-four inches tall and his hard hat covered most of his face. He looked like a little kid playing dress up. Louis and Ed stood by silently while Burt interrogated us about the stolen tools. There was a power-struggle brewing before anyone said a word. Large construction jobs are rife with attitude as different parties vie for position. Companies want to hire their own crews at the same time the Union is trying to keep people in their local communities working. Company-men tend to focus on finishing one job and starting the next. In my experience, they are often paranoid, easily threatened and hard to trust. I was hoping for an exception. Burt wasn't it.

"We got ripped off again." Burt said. "They didn't take any personal tools, as usual. Every gang box we have on the job got hit so we ain't got no power tools. Somebody had a key. You people set this up to stop work. Who has the key for this gang box? Which one of you people locked up on Friday?" He looked directly at me.

I said nothing and smiled.

Burt turned to Kevin. "Who locked up on Friday?"

"I did. I'm the key-man for the crew." Kevin replied confidently. "We were all here and Teddy checked the lock as he always does."

"Figures. Was there anybody else here to, you know, verify your story?"

"Watch it Burt!" Ed cut in. "If they say they locked up then they did! Unlimited is always laying people off without collecting the keys. Why don't you change the locks like I told you the first time this happened? It's no wonder stuff gets ripped off. Maybe you could be the key-man for this entire job!"

"No fucking way! We got a-hundred gang boxes on this site. I'd spend all day looking for lockups! Nobody could get any work done 'till I found them. You Union people are getting away with murder. We need a company-man on every crew," Burt yelled.

"You need to get the hell away from my men," the carpenter steward announced as he marched toward them. "You're not bringin' in any more men from outta state. And if you want to stay here another three years, you're gonna have to abide by the rules of THIS region." Smitty was staring down at Burt, whose eyes were level with Smitty's chest.

"Then somebody has got to go." Burt stomped off.

Smitty came over to examine the loss. "Who opened up this morning?"

Ed answered. "We came up with Burt. The box was open then."

"And you locked up on Friday?" He asked the brothers.

"Yea, and Teddy checked it." Kevin spoke while Teddy and I nodded.

I was trying to grasp the meaning of the situation while we put on our tool belts. "I never heard of such a thing. You mean to tell me that somebody came in over the weekend and cleaned out all the gang boxes? Somebody with a key? How'd they get all that stuff out of here! Screw guns, nail guns, skill-saws. And they didn't touch any personal tools?"

Smitty answered. "Well, no one from Unlimited worked this weekend. Other companies worked, but down in the mall part of the job. People do change companies pretty quick around here. Anybody can get keys to any

19

lock-up they want. It clearly wasn't you guys, or gal, but it had to be somebody who knew their way around here pretty damn well."

"I guess we'll be going, huh?" Teddy suggested. "Burt's been waiting for a chance like this."

"We'll see about that. You guys just hang tight and do the best you can," Ed said. He walked off with Smitty.

"This is just crazy." I was still confused. "What the hell are we supposed to do without any power tools?"

"Look bad! Burt would just love to come up here and find us not working. Don't let them do that to you sister. We'll cut studs all day if we have to," Keven explained.

"You mean we gotta cut studs for the sake of cutting studs?" I asked.

"It's all politics," Teddy replied. "They can get everything we need in less than an hour if they want. It's up to them. But we gotta do our part."

Kevin's eyes lit up. "We still have our radio. We'll just have to make rough cuts for now. When the screw guns arrive, we can hop right up there and knock it out. I'd like to knock out Burt." We all laughed.

We cut studs until lunchtime, and still no power tools. The floor was cluttered with piles of scraps, and our hands ached from using tin-snips all morning. I took breaks to stack the staging with cut pieces to give my blisters a rest.

Burt was waiting at our gang box after lunch. "You guys are all late."

Kevin looked at his watch. "You know we're always at the elevator on time, and that it takes about five minutes to get up here."

20

"Then walk!" Burt snapped. "I'm working with you guys from now on."

Teddy wandered back to the side he'd been working on. His load was lighter without any power tools.

Kevin and I put on our tool belts. "Me and Jean are partners but you could stock us up if you want."

"You'll do what I tell you!" Burt yelled. He started to quiver.

Kevin and I left him standing there talking to himself as we went to our work area. Burt pointed to me. "You come with me," he demanded.

"HEY!" Kevin butted in. "You want a partner then go get your own. I need her, so screw, Burt!"

"I can't. No screw gun." Burt nearly smiled.

From across the atrium Ed came trotting over.

"Knock your shit off, Burt, and get the hell outta here. Go count screws or something, but do it away from my men! Maybe somebody's looking for you on the 35th floor." Ed walked past Burt, and gave me and Kevin a new screw gun. "These are assigned to you by serial number. Don't let them outta your sight. Don't lend them to anyone cause you're each responsible for your own guns from now on." Ed looked directly at Burt as he explained the breakdown of new equipment. He also gave Kevin a new lock and nail gun, and put him in charge of both.

"So where's mine?" Burt demanded.

"Go ask your father-in-law. He made the list, and gave me these to hand out." Ed walked away smiling.

"What am I supposed to do?" Burt asked again, empty-handed.

"Cut studs." I suggested, and started reading off measurements for Burt to cut.

Kevin leaned over to me. "You're pushing it."

I smiled as Burt stomped out.

We fell into the rhythm of our work and almost finished one side when Burt returned. He was not alone. He marched up to me and ordered me to give him my screw gun. I looked at him, and then to the men with him. Then I looked at Kevin.

"Gimme your gun, girl!"

I ignored him so he yelled louder. "I said give me your gun, damn it. Now!"

Kevin cut in. "You afraid to say that to me Burt? Come over here and try to take my screw gun."

Burt's face deepened in shades of red. He glared at me, sucking in air as if it would make him tall enough to look me in the eye. I did not respond. He unplugged my extension cord from the wall and yanked it toward him. The cord was tied to the staging and the jolt brought me to my knees on the platform. I grabbed the cord and pulled it back. The two of us played tug-of-war with the extension cord like children. It was one of those moments when you have to decide who you really are. Rather than fight him I let the cord go. He lost his balance and fell into the pile of metal scraps and trash on the floor. I wanted to lunge at him from the staging platform but I caught myself. My rage was full of fury from past indignities and it scared me. Being overpowered by inflated ego was familiar and I had to keep myself in check. Sure, Burt's behavior was dangerous, but the sanctioned violence done to me as a child was bigger than any one man. I had to stay present. I didn't want to be the woman on the job who beat up the owner's son-in-law. I didn't want to beat up anyone. I was overwhelmed and tired of feeling stuck between victim and survivor.

Everybody was laughing and I knew then that no one would stop me if I directed my rage. I backed off still yelling. "What the fuck is your problem? You little chickenshit! Get some therapy, asshole!"

Burt was beet read. "I don't need no damn therapy!"

"That's what you think!" I turned and headed for the women's bathroom. Muttering to myself, *I can't let him reduce me to his level,* until my breathing evened out. I was still muttering obscenities as I entered the women's bathroom.

"Excuse me..." A deep voice echoed in the empty room.

I saw no one, and slammed the door shut behind me.

The voice bellowed again. "I'm working in here. AAh.... Hello. Do you want me to leave?"

"Even in the woman's bathroom I can't get away from you guys!" I exclaimed to the unfamiliar voice. "Who's in here? I noticed the cords and followed them. I heard the Zing of a screw gun, and then silence.

Out of the last stall appeared a tall black man with white sheetrock dust all over his face. Seeing him made me realize he was the first black worker from Unlimited I had met. "Do you want me to step outside?" He put his hands up and started to back out. I was shocked by his immediate defensive response. I wasn't threatened by him at all and his reaction felt so real it made me sad.

"No thanks. I'm just hiding out for a few minutes. You work for Unlimited?"

"Yea, I'm Robby." He smiled. "And you must be Jean, the only female sheetrocker on the entire site," he laughed. "The entire city probably." We both relaxed as our banter became casual. Being the only one gave us something in common.

"Yea, that's me. I feel like I work in a fishbowl sometimes, or that I'm some kind of experiment with all this curiosity and all."

"I bet. I mean, I know. Before it was you, it was me." Robby looked directly at me with a knowing smile.

"Yea, I reckon you're right there. Where's your partner?"

"What partner? People like me don't get partners. Sometimes I'm a baby sitter so it's not always a bad thing." His laugh sounded hearty, sincere and very wise.

We chatted for a bit more before I headed back to my post. Talking with Robby was comforting. We were up against the same haters although for different reasons. I was often partnered with black men, which was presented as a game. There was an assumption that, as a white woman, I would be afraid to work alone with a black man for eight hours a day. I wasn't. The ignorance and bias actually worked in our favor. My partners of color were better teachers than most of my white partners and they weren't threatened by my presence.

Burt was gone when I returned. "What did you guys do with Burt?"

"We didn't have to do anything. I was kind of hoping you'd take him out," Kevin snickered.

"I have worked very hard to ward off bullies without becoming one."

Teddy laughed. "That was before you met Burt!" He gathered his supplies and returned to his side of the atrium. Kevin and I switched our conversation to the task at hand and continued with the rhythm of our work. At two-thirty Smitty showed up.

Teddy was the first to greet him. "You got our checks?" He joked.

"Yea, two of them. Sorry, but Burt's in Unlimited's shack raising hell." Smitty handed each of them their lay-off check.

"Please keep Burt away from me!" I begged Smitty, half-laughing.

"I hope you can hold your own sister, 'cause you may get stuck with him tomorrow." Smitty answered.

"He's dangerous," I reminded him.

Smitty wandered back toward me as he spoke. "Don't forget, you're an apprentice, and he is who he is...for what it's worth."

"So!"

Smitty smiled. "I can't push my luck. Besides, lots of men are leaving today. We gotta take it easy for a while. I'm with you all the way. If he acts up, then we'll be able to do something about it. One day, that's all I ask. If he hurts you then you can screw him to the wall."

25

"IF HE HURTS ME?" Wow, that didn't need time to sink in.

The Wood brothers were packing up their tools, getting ready to depart. I was sad to see them go.

Teddy spoke first. "Good luck to you, Jean. We know you're gonna need it.

"You're good at your trade, sister, remember that," Kevin said. We all shook hands and in an instant they were gone.

Standing alone on the vacant floor, I watched them walk away until the elevator gates crashed shut behind them. I shuffled around in the clutter of metal scraps on the floor. The stillness around me was comforting but the uncertainty of what, or whom, came next was equally unsettling. I've been in this place before; on my own trying to figure out where I fit in. The outsider...The only one...The one who got too much attention for being who I am...Trying to make peace with things we can't talk about...A survivor of a reality I did not have words to describe.

I spent the last hour organizing the gang box, looking over the work yet to be done; and considering different tactics for dealing with Burt. I was already dreading him. I wrapped up the cords, radio, and the screw guns; slammed the gang box shut, and kicked it for spite. If he hurts me indeed.

Shit Gets Real

Another day. Another partner. I waited for the others in Unlimited's shack and, after ripping the pornography off the interior walls, sat down with my thermos of coffee. I recognized some of the workers coming in, stocking up, and leaving. Ed appeared and sat across from me. From the look on his face I was prepared for a lecture but his calm tone made me realize I was off the hook.

"So you haven't done much rockin'?" He asked in a paternal way.

"Not industrial. I have done residential sheetrock but nothing like this. I understand the procedure but I haven't had the chance to practice much."

"Well, you're gonna get the chance now. I don't like to see you girls hanging board if I can set you up framing but Burt is out to kill you. You and Robby should work out alright though. He's a good rocker, and smart for... He'll teach you a lot and I doubt he'll give you any trouble."

Robby came in and sat down with us.

I turned to face him. "Howdy partner. You and me huh?"

He smiled back and turned to Ed. "Where we working?"

"Ask Burt. He's your foreman now," Ed replied.

"I guess we can't have everything." Robby said and we all laughed.

27

Burt stuck his head in the door. "Vacation's over. Let's go!"

In a very sympathetic voice Ed wished me and Robby good luck.

The three of us walking out were a very different trio than me and the Wood brothers and I missed them a lot just then. Burt marched ahead, empty handed. Robby and I followed along with our tools.

When we neared the elevator Robby was the first to speak. "Where are we working, Burt?"

Burt waved for us to follow him but Robby stopped by the elevator and put his tools down. Burt turned back toward us. "What the fuck do you think you're doing?"

"That's what I just asked you. We got all our tools here. What floor are we working on?" Robby stood his ground for both of us.

Burt looked at me. "I guess you're going to need all the help you can get. Up to twelve," and he took off for the stairs.

I looked at Robby and grumbled as I pushed the UP button. We got on and greeted the operator. "Where's Freddy today?"

"Out sick I guess." The operator tipped his head toward Robby and gave me a knowing nod as we stepped in. I had no idea what he thought he knew but I didn't think it was good. I shrugged back.

Once we got to the twelfth floor, Robby and I walked through a maze of dark corridors to the atrium where we waited for Burt. I was taken aback by the fact that I didn't recognize where we were. I had worked on the twelfth floor before but nothing around me looked familiar. Suddenly the job seemed even bigger than before. There were now walls going up, twenty feet high and framed with metal studs. Not only was there no one in sight but there was a desolate feeling to the dimly lit space.

Burt came from the opposite side of the atrium with the gang box and a few new faces. Company men Robby explained, six of them plus Burt.

"You're probably the best of the lot," he added.

"I hope that's a compliment!"

"Sorta," he smirked.

"Well thanks anyway," we both chuckled. In another setting that could have been insulting. But this kind of banter cuts the tension when you have to put your safety in the hands of a stranger. Robby and I were still feeling each other out. Our pairing could go either way. It was oddly comforting that I felt so akin to someone who was different from me in so many ways.

Robby switched to a serious tone. "They're gonna be watching us pretty closely. The whole job will be talking about us being partners if you know what I mean."

"Oh please." I groaned, knowing exactly what he meant. "I once heard a rumor that I got laid-off to have my foreman's baby. Can you imagine that?" *If they only knew...* I thought to myself as I stuffed my reality as far down as possible.

"Thanks for bringing up the gang box, Burt." I greeted him cordially.

His buddies snickered and snorted.

Burt turned his back to me. Clearly enjoying the power he had over us, he divided up the other workers. "Jack, Steve and Bill-you guys work out here, on the atrium side of the wall. Take the east side." He pointed north. "Hank, Mike, and Dougie can start at the other end. We're doing tops." Burt turned to us. "Salt and Pepper, you two work in the back corridor. And you can start at either end." He started to walk away before he finished talking to us.

Robby yelled after him. "So me and her are doing the same work as three journeymen?"

Burt stopped and turned. With hands on his hips he replied. "I know you got your handicaps but do the best you can. I don't expect nothing from youse-two anyway. That's why I got you working in the back corridor." He turned again and walked away.

I looked at Robby. "What just happened?"

"Fuck him girl. Let's go. God damn racist shit. I hope you can hang board, sister."

"You'll be the first to know but I'll give it my best shot. Ed and Louis know my sheetrock experience is limited, and Smitty does too. I really don't care what Burt thinks. I'm not trying to pick a fight with you but I think he's full of sexist shit too."

Robby looked at me with a smile that hinted at more than it said, but did not feel condescending. "Girl, he's too busy hating me to care about hating you. And besides, nobody is taking you seriously anyway. That's why they put you with me. Damn fools don't see how their little white ego trips hurt everybody. You'll see what I mean if they keep us together."

He laughed at the look on my face. I just couldn't wrap my head around being hurt by white racism.

Robbie continued. "White supremacy isn't just about racism. It's about white people thinking they are superior because they inherited the right to call the shots and hold that over the rest of us. Hell, you gotta worry about people who claim to have discovered a new land after they killed off the people who greeted them. Then they kidnapped people from another continent to maintain the land that they just stole. It's pitiful that we teach our kids to be proud of that history!"

I didn't know what to make of this. I was taken off guard that he spoke so frankly about racism with me. It struck me how much I didn't get it because I was on the winning team. I didn't need to understand what he said to trust he knew what he was talking about. Something clicked for me though. I thought of the ways people assumed control of my life or ignored physical boundaries to take what they want. I never thought of it as white supremacy, but he had a point. "Well, I can't argue with you." I replied sincerely.

"Smart girl, um, woman, whatever. As far as our work is concerned, I only ask that you try. I don't care if you can or you can't, as long as you try. I'll work you as hard as you let me, and then some. There's not much to it, but tops are tough. I've worked with a lot of apprentices and I'll help you all I can, but if you wimp out on me you're on your own. I won't go easy on you because you're a girl either. You want the pay you gotta earn it. Don't get me wrong, I'm not a mean bastard but I just want you to know where I'm coming from. Alright?"

"Fine," I agreed. "I want to do this. You're gonna have to explain the breakdown to me if you don't mind."

"I don't mind. It works better if we both work the same plan. Usually three people work tops but this has the making of a true adventure." His chuckle was comforting. "We're doing tops because the walls are twenty feet high and the sheetrock is only twelve feet long. A previous crew hung these twelve-footers and our job is to sheetrock above that, from the twelve-footer to the ceiling. That's what we call the tops. When journeymen work as partners we usually switch jobs. One guy cuts and the other uh...guy measures and screws off the sheet. Since you're an apprentice, you're going to be screwing off for a while just so you can get the hang of it, so to speak. Ha Ha."

We unpacked our tool buckets and loaded our belts while he talked about the work we were about to do.

Robby walked over to a six-foot section of staging, waving me towards another one. We rolled them to our post, wheeling around piles of sheetrock, metal studs, and mounds of trash on the floor. Once we arrived at our post I said, "Ummm. I don't do well with my feet off the ground." I didn't realize how much I was hoping for sympathy until I didn't get it.

"You'll have to forget about that while you're up there." Robby chuckled as he climbed up on the first platform. "Break that one down, and pass me the sections. Please. Always be the one who assembles the staging you'll be working on."

I took the sections of the staging apart and passed them up to Robby. He added them to the staging he was on to make the second level. "It's gettin' to be coffee time. How 'bout I go before we get too involved here. I can't believe we aren't even set up yet and it is already time for coffee..."

"Don't bother with the others. I need you, and they're each working in teams of three. Fuck 'em!" He handed me a five dollar bill and asked for a coffee and glazed donut. "Use the change for whatever you're getting. On me."

Robby had everything set up when I returned and we sat on a stack of sheetrock to have our coffee.

Out of nowhere Burt appeared. He glared at me. "Aren't you going for coffee?"

"I just did. See?" I raised my coffee to show him.

"What about the men?"

Robby stood and towered over Burt. "Oh, you mean the trios? Why should we fetch for them when they get an extra man? Maybe one of THEM should get coffee for us." Robby suggested, reminding Burt that his division of labor was obvious.

"But she's the gir, the apprentice," Burt countered.

I stood and cast a shadow onto Burt from the other side. "And yet I can work like one and a half journeymen, when I'm not getting coffee like a 'gir-apprentice.'"

"You get everybody's coffee from now on!" Burt marched out.

"Ignore him Jean. I got half a nerve to go over there and step on him. Who does he think he is? I don't know if he's trying to kill YOU or ME. I hope you're ready for

33

this, girl, I mean, woman. Isn't that what you'd rather be called?"

"You can call me Snow White if you say it nicely."

He laughed. "OK Snow White, this is it. Get up there. Too bad Boston Blackie was a white guy, Ha Ha."

"Do I have to," I whined as I carried my tools over to the staging.

Robby handed me a screw gun. "When you're screwing off the sheets, don't hold the gun by the handle. He showed me how he gripped his screw gun for the rapid succession required to screw off a sheet. "Lucky for you, you have big hands. He offered me a gallant smile. "Ok sister. Get up there. You got screws? Tape measure? Utility Knife? Little sheetrock saw?"

"Got 'em." I started to climb up the outside of the staging. "Isn't there something else you need to tell me before I go up there? Did I tell you how much I hate working heights?"

"I can see that from the way you're avoiding the top HA HA HA. Just be careful. You won't fall. I'll catch you if you do." Robby was laughing and our banter was fun and easy. "Come on now. You can do it but you gotta do it today."

"Alright alright alright!" I finally got from the side of the staging to the platform on top. I froze as the staging wobbled beneath me. I couldn't stand up straight without weaving my body between the ducts, pipes and conduits coming from every direction.

Robby couldn't see me so he yelled. "Are you ready? I'm gonna mark the sheetrock so you know where the studs are once you get the sheet up there. We can't assume anything about the framing since we didn't do it so I need you to verify the spacing of the studs. Then I'll need the length. OKAY?"

"Got it. Here ya go. Fourteen. Thirty-one. Forty-eight. Length, ninety-two and a half. That's tight. Do you want the lengths loose or tight?" I was yelling from above. Good thing he knew to check since the wall hadn't been framed correctly.

"Read me tight for now, and I'll make the adjustments. Check both edges for the lengths, just in case the deck above isn't even."

"I did," I confirmed, proud that I thought of that before he mentioned it.

"Are you ready, Jean?"

"As ready as I'll ever be." I got into position, squatting on the staging close to the wall but not sure what to expect.

Robby put the sheet on the first section of staging and joined it there. This is where the third worker comes in, I realized as he climbed up to the staging platform so he could pass the sheet up to me. "Okay Snow White, get ready."

I felt like a bull in a bullring, planting and replanting my feet while shaking my head.

"Here's what you do," he continued. "Grab the sheet on the sides when I slide it up the wall. Good. Okay. Good. Now, when you stand up, the sheet will come up with you. I'm letting go now so you're in control of the sheet. That's good. You got it. Now toss it up, slide your hands along the side edges while you kneel back down to grab a lower hold on the sheet. You repeat that until you can rest the sheet up on the staging platform." He seemed to have more confidence in me than I did.

"Say what?"

Robbie laughed. "You're kinda skinny so you might have to do that a few times to get the sheet all the way up. But then again, you're tall so that's in your favor."

"Alrighty then. You better get outta the way." We were still yelling back and forth to be heard.

As I stood up, I threw my momentum into tossing the sheet even higher. I quickly knelt again to get a lower grip on the sheet. The next time I stood up I raised the sheet high enough to rest it on the staging platform. "Mother of god!" I gasped when I landed the sheet in front of me. I looked down to Robby. "You have got to be kidding!"

"Not bad for a skinny kid," he chuckled. "You got the hang of it, as we say in the trade. Ha, ha. It just takes practice. You ready to put the sheet into place?"

"I'm ready to go home," I whined back.

He rightfully ignored that. "Okay. First you've got to get your screw gun ready. Put it in your pouch with a screw on it. Now, slide the sheet up the studs above of the bottom sheet. Good. Good. When you get the sheet high enough, tilt the bottom in and rest it on the sheet beneath it. You can use your foot where the sheets come together so it won't slip. Then use your body to push the sheet against the studs. Be careful. You got less than an inch to land the sheet on. You got it...You got it. Now, keep your foot there and rock the sheet over so it's tight against the other one. GENTLY. Good. Now tack it off with two or three screws and read me the measurements for the next sheet. You can screw off that one while I'm marking the next one. If you have to climb onto the heat duct to screw off the top, stand on the edge so the duct won't buckle under you."

I tacked-off the sheet, pulled out my tape measure and gave Robby the next set of measurements. I picked up my screw gun and a handful of screws. It was very dark that close to the ceiling but Robby's marks were easy to follow. There was a rhythm in the task but I hadn't found it yet. Though my part was fairly simple, mastering each step was crucial. One false move and one or the other of us could get seriously hurt. Working on the doubled-up staging gave me the willies, and dancing with seventy pounds of sheetrock up there kept me aware of my surroundings.

Robby had already marked and cut the next sheet, and was patiently waiting.

"Sorry to keep ya," I said when I realized.

"No problem. You'll pick up speed. You ready? Remember the last time."

Robby placed the sheet on the staging platform, climbed onto the first platform and started to slide it up the wall.

"Oh shit. You don't waste a minute do ya?" I knelt to get ahold of the sheet. I see it, I got it. I got it." I stood up with the sheet, and after a few grunts I set it on the platform in front of me. Each motion was felt by the wobbly staging as I moved the awkward weight around. And I hated it. "Like it grew there," I yelled as the sheetrock landed perfectly into place. "Can I go home now?"

"Can you afford it?"

"Always the wise guy."

"And that's why they pay me the big money," he laughed.

"If you can make a sheetrocker out of me you deserve the big money!" We both laughed.

We did pretty well that morning as a mutual respect grew between us. At ten to twelve, Robby told me to come down for lunch.

We left our tool belts on the first platform of the staging, and walked out with the others for lunch.

Burt was standing by our staging when we returned. "You guys left early."

Ignoring him, I put on my tools and restocked the staging.

Robby turned to Burt. "Don't just stand there, be our middle man. You can get on the first section, and I'll pass the sheet to you." Burt left without another word.

Robby called me over and pointed to the pile of wing nuts on the floor. "Call me crazy, but I want you to check the braces on our staging."

I looked where the braces were attached to sections of staging. "Well, don't that beat all. Is this what you call a coincidental mechanical failure or is it what I think it is?" The braces were still there but the nuts that locked them in place were gone. The braces would have worked loose by the end of the day. Someone was messing with us.

We screwed the wing nuts back on and looked blankly at each other. What can you say when something like that happens? The fear that threatens to overwhelm you embeds itself in a place you dare not go.

Robby was first to speak. "We're gonna have to find more board somewhere."

"Don't we have laborers for that sort of thing?"

"There are only three laborers here for seventy-five carpenters."

"Unlimited has seventy-five carpenters? Where are the rest of them hiding? Shouldn't there be one laborer for every crew?"

"Girl, you may be good at your trade, but you got a lot to learn about construction. There's also supposed to be ten percent women and minorities. What we are is what they got! We just gotta take our time, that's all. They can play their little games with us all they want but they won't win. And we've got to choose our battles wisely. After what just happen to our staging-do you think anyone cares if we have to get our own stock?"

We finished our wall. Burt watched as I put the last few screws into place. "You two come with me. I got another job for you."

Robby and I packed up our tools and followed him. Nobody spoke. We finished the day at our new post. The next morning found us there again, and many mornings after.

* * * * * *

"I HATE THIS! Give me a break," I yelled from above.

Robby knew I needed to blow off steam so he didn't take offense. I knew his laughter was the same for him and not done in malice either. "I sure can hear ya, but I can't see ya. Yo, Jean? Are you alright up there? Talk to me. How's it going?" Robby was peering around from below trying to see me.

"It's a good thing I like you, 'cause I'm cursing your ass right now. There just isn't enough room up here for me with all this ductwork, conduit and drain pipes everywhere. There's no light, and all this fuzzy fireproofing stuff is itching inside my shirt. I'm a cutter he says. Sure you are," I finished sarcastically.

Robby really did sympathize with me, but the fit I was having made him laugh. "I feel your pain sister, I really do, but you are entertaining. Honestly, I thought it would take you longer to get up to speed. Just don't take your frustrations out on the work or on your partner." We had developed a safe but guarded comradery from enduring this together. In spite of, or maybe because of our differences, we knew we needed each other to make the best of this bad situation.

"Okay I'm done. Get me the hell outta here." I started singing. "What kind of fool do you think I am?"

"Okay, but where are you?" Robby looked up as one lone leg emerged and slid down the wall toward the top platform. "That's it. Easy does it. Come straight down."

"For the love of god! This is downright pitiful!" I hopped off the heating duct onto the top platform of the

40

staging. We had been working in the most dreadful place of all, the utility room. Hanging sheetrock wasn't nearly as tiresome as the preparation for each section. It was hot working so close to all the rumbling machinery; and too dark and noisy to communicate easily. But we could curse our frustrations out on each other then turn around and laugh about it, which we did. It can take all you've got to maintain a productive attitude working in such an area ten hours a day. I liked to sing to take the edge off and Robby didn't complain since he couldn't hear me over the noise.

Once again we took the staging apart and set it up further down the wall.

"I don't know if I can survive another week here. Wouldn't it be fair for everyone to spend time here?"

"There you go with that fair stuff again," he laughed. You can say something to Ed if you want, but don't get your hopes up. Who knows? He can only say no."

"Or laugh in my face. You know, Ed has been scarce around here lately."

Robby agreed. "Yea, I noticed."

I had to squeeze around, up and over ductwork, to reach the top of the wall.

My eyes haven't adjusted. "I can't see shit up here."

"Look around long enough and I bet you will," Robby assured me. The visual implication of his remark struck me. I had been on construction sites long enough to know that possibility first hand. "Did you have to say that?"

Robby cut the sheet to length then into smaller pieces so we could maneuver them around the machinery and duct work. Because these walls would never be seen, it didn't matter how they looked. He put the pieces onto the first level of the staging and climbed up to pass them up to me. Wise enough to choose his battles; Robby was doing the work of the cutter and the middle man with such grace.

I put the pieces of sheetrock on the top platform and screwed one into place. Then I put the other pieces on the heating duct and climbed up onto it. The ductwork was less stable than the staging so the slightest motion pushed me and the duct away from the wall, terrifying me. "Mother of god, I don't believe I'm up here doing this."

"Neither do I..." The voice wasn't Robby's. I couldn't place it.

"Who's down there laughing at me now?" I finished screwing off the sheet while voices below talked about me. Back down on the staging, I called out. "You guys want a weather report from up here, or WHAT? Oh, hi Louis. Hi Smitty. Don't mind me. It's the lack of oxygen."

Louis's mouth was wide open. He was dumbfounded. Smitty had a pleased grin on his face and Robby stood back taking it all in.

"What the hell are you doing up there, Jean?" Smitty asked.

"I'm gettin' high. Care to join me?"

"Burt's been at it again I see. Come on down. You two were supposed to be outta here weeks ago. I've been looking all over for you."

I started the precarious descent to the floor. "I'm sorry Smitty; I'm really doing my best. I can't see and it takes forever to..."

"Relax, honey. It's okay. Burt was supposed to switch you guys. Everybody has to do equal time in the utility rooms. Where is that little weasel?"

"He doesn't come around here anymore. Maybe his conscience is getting the best of him," Robby said.

"Sheee-it," was all I said.

"I'm pleased that you two stuck it out. I'll make up for this. Good work, both of you. Wait until I get my hands on that little bastard."

"Can I watch?" I pleaded jokingly.

Together the four of us found Burt having coffee with the company men. Robby and I continued towards him, while Smitty stayed back with Louis to listen.

Burt stood up. "What the fuck are you guys doing here? What's the matter? Can't she take it? "

"We're all done." Robby cut him off.

"WHAT? I don't believe it! You finished all the utility rooms? You gotta be shitting me?"

Robby looked at the others before he replied, "We wouldn't shit you Burt. You're our favorite turd!" Smitty and Louis burst out laughing as they walked toward us.

Burt swelled up like a puffer fish. Robby was laughing and Louis was mumbling and pointing. He laughed so hard his hammer hoop squeaked. I backed away.

Smitty stepped in. "So shorty, what's your excuse this time? I told you everybody does time in the utility rooms. These guys have done their time and they will NOT return! YOU GOT THAT? GOOD." He turned to one of the trios. "You three finish up in there. I want my girl here to get a chance at some of the fancy stuff. And they have both earned it! Put them on knee walls until I tell you otherwise. That's it. Coffee's over!" Smitty waved for Louis to follow him out.

You Said I Could

"You and me, buddy. I'm almost excited about working today. I can't believe that we finally got a job without endless obstacles. And on a Monday no less! Something funny is going on. If I'm dreaming, don't wake me. Let me enjoy it for a while."

"Do you know what to do?" Robby asked.

"Yea, but point me in the right direction; I'm not sure where to do it."

Robby pointed to the edge of the atrium.

"Oh, yea, we've got to measure back." I saw comparisons to making light pockets with Kevin as we put on our tool belts and reviewed the blueprints.

The entire day passed without interference. It was startling to realize how much of our workday had been wasted because Burt didn't need *no damn therapy.*

We arranged our work around the sun as the skylight magnified the heat and the glare. The plasterers were working above us in the atrium on the center staging. Every now and then a glob of wet plaster would SPLAT next to us on the floor.

We finished the layout and framing in good time. We were halfway through the thirteenth floor when our job got changed again. Smitty came by and talked to Robby before he turned to me. "I need you to work with Danny for a few days. You'll be back on knee-walls with Robby next week. Promise."

Danny was a character that I had met on a picket line. When we met at the gang-box the next morning he greeted me with, "Oh shit. You're a broad."

I said nothing and smiled.

"You're coming with me, baby."

"You start calling me Your Woman and I'm out of here." I laughed, hoping to set a firm boundary at first chance.

Robby laughed, and shook his head. "Good luck Jean. I'll be seeing you..."

"In all the Oooold familiar places." I sang.

"You two got something going?" Danny inquired as we walked away. Without waiting for an answer he continued, "This way, baby."

We carried our tools, cords, and screw guns to the back hallway and set up to work. The area was already framed and the sheetrock was stacked nearby. I was relieved. That meant we were not doing tops. I plugged in the cords, and Danny kicked the studs around until I had everything ready.

"I cut. You screw. I bet you like screwing don't you?" Danny said with a smirk. He marked the twelve-foot-long sheet, and I helped him hoist it upright. We walked the sheet over and leaned it up against the studs. I was poised and ready as I read the bubbles in my level. Once the sheet was lined up he tacked it into place. ZING ZING ZING. All this took about three minutes. Danny set up the next sheet while I screwed off the first one. I had to use a ladder to reach the top of the twelve foot sheet.

46

Danny had the second sheet ready before I finished. He had walked it over and leaned it against the first one. He was yelling for me to come down from the ladder and tack this one into place. "Come down here and screw me." I kept shaking my head to shake off the way he spoke to me. I finished the first sheet and climbed down. I said nothing, but started to tack off the next sheet. That was all there was to it. Mark the sheet, walk it over, and screw it off. I was grateful that the constant sound of the screw gun's ZING eliminated any room for conversation. I could put my work on cruise control but that was the easy part of the job. Learning a trade we aren't raised to consider was hard enough, but women in nontraditional jobs have an additional challenge; confronting the toxic attitude masking fragile masculinity. It wears you down so slowly that you don't realize how much energy it takes until your tolerance dwindles. Suddenly you notice your own behavior with clenching fists. Gritting your teeth, you try to reason with someone that plays pocket pool with his scrotum and talks to your breasts. It is an endless battle. I listened to the little voice inside me that was stronger than all of them. It kept repeating itself. Consider the source! Consider the source! Consider the source! It would emerge in appropriate little ditties, and usually just in time. But there's always the guy that tries your patience like a persistent mosquito buzzing near your ear. "I sure like the view from down here. You got a nice ass, baby." Danny was cupping his crotch as he walked towards me.

I tried to ignore him but my guard went up. There was no one around and this joker could do as he pleased. I didn't trust him and they'd never find my body until the building opened. *Where is Smitty when I need him? He got me into this.* I pushed the screw gun harder trying to drown Danny out with the noise. ZING. ZING. ZING.

Danny continued with his comments. "You can't take a compliment can you? You one of them broads with no sense of humor? Let your hair down some. Maybe we can have a little fun. I don't know if I can control myself working with you all day. What does your boyfriend think about you screwing with men for work?"

He held up the next sheet and I tacked it off. I was seething and struggling to ease my mind so that I could work safely as I stepped onto the ladder. His remarks and hungry looks were beating me down. I kept pushing the screws harder and harder and Danny kept pushing me closer and closer to the edge with his comments. How can I make them realize that this kind of harassment affects workplace safety? I looked down at my ladder, and then stepped onto the tread that warned: DO NOT STAND ON OR ABOVE THIS STEP... With the screw gun in my hand and a fist full of screws, I reached over to screw off the very top of the sheet. As I leaned, so did Danny. Our eyes locked and I felt trouble coming. I had no time to avoid it. Just as I stretched to sink the last screw, he reached up and grabbed my crotch full in his hand. We both went down. I landed on the concrete slab on top of Danny and the ladder landed on top of me. I was dazed and laid there as he wriggled out from underneath me. I looked at my hand and saw blood from where the screws had stabbed into my palm. "You made me bleed."

Danny bent over to pick up the ladder as I lay there twisting screws out of my hand. The coating on the screws stung a little. He just stood there grinning as he unzipped his fly. The moment froze in my mind. He was so pleased with himself. I watched his hands unbuckle his belt and my mind went blank. ZING ZING ZING. Next thing I know I was rolling away from the wall and Danny was flailing in place. I didn't realize I had screwed his pants to the wall until I heard the screws connect with a stud. He was attached to the wall with his tighty-whities exposed for everyone to see.

"Hey bitch! What the fuck are you doing? You fucking cunt!" Danny was yelling.

"You kept asking me to screw you so I did." I got to my feet. I was just as surprised as he was that I reacted so quickly. I was also nauseous from realizing what could have happened if I didn't. I threw-up in a pile of scrap on my way to the intercom.

Danny was thrashing and yelling. "Where are you going? Hey, don't leave me here. Where are you going, bitch? Let me down." He was pleading. "Come back here you motherfucking cunt! You can't do this. I'm gonna...."

"Who's sorry now?" I turned and sang before lifting the intercom. I could hear my shaky voice echo through the building, "Smitty, and Ed from Unlimited... Please report to thirteen, uhh, Smitty and Ed to thirteen. Back corridor. Asap."

Robby was the first to appear. "What's up, Jean? I heard you... What the hell happened here?" He started to laugh so hard he doubled over. "I knew something had to be up, but I never thought it would be Danny, stuck up on the wall. You holding up the building, Danny? Oh this is going to be good." Robby leaned against the wall close enough to Danny to taunt him. "You're ok, right Jean? He didn't...?"

I shook my head *no.*

Smitty came rushing over first. "What's the matter? Somebody get hurt?" He focused immediately on the blood on the floor, and then to my hand, which I had completely forgotten about. He looked at Danny twice before it hit him. "What's HE doing like THAT?"

"When Ed gets here I'll fill you in.

"Let him down," Smitty suggested.

"When he confesses he's a free man. And I want witnesses! Ed will be right along."

Ed trotted over and noticed Danny first thing. His hand went to his forehead. "I've seen it all now. You're supposed to hang sheetrock, girl, not your partner. What the hell?"

"Well." I turned to Danny. "Tell him what happened, Danny. Tell 'em how it happened and I'll let you down. Oh DannyBoy, I long to free you..."

"Bitch was falling so I caught her," he mumbled.

"You saved her and she screwed you to the wall?" Robby laughed. "Sounds screwy to me, if you don't mind the pun."

I stepped in. "Let's just get it over with. Fess up."

"You let me down first, bitch!" Danny demanded.

"You're in no position to negotiate. I got the only screw gun." ZING ZING. I played with the trigger to tease him. Smitty reached for my screw gun but I pulled back.

"So big deal, I touched your leg." Danny was trying to kick himself free.

Ed walked over to him and spoke quietly. "I find that hard to believe. Did you cop a feel or something worse?" Ed glanced at Danny's unzipped pants. "You were in deep shit before this happened, and I know better than to argue with a pissed off broad with the only screw gun."

Robby butted in next. "I think you owe my friend an apology."

"What? Me apologize to THAT CUNT? NEVER!"

I smiled at my hostage. "He's been begging me to screw him, so I did. Well boys, I've got work to do." I went over to the cart, and started to mark the next sheet. Smitty and Ed chatted, and Robby turned to leave.

Danny freaked out and started screaming. "Hey. You can't get away with this. Don't leave me here."

"Face it Danny boy. You're gonna have to fess up sooner or later. Tell the fellas how you pushed me off the ladder when you assaulted me."

"You know I didn't assault you. I just graaa... You fell. You're dead now you motherfucking bitch. Bro code, ya know? Us guys will stick together. You'll see." Danny was weary, and hung his head. "I should have jumped your ass while I had the chance."

"Look Danny, none of these guys have tools on. I don't like you as it is. You could rot here for all I care. I'm getting tired of looking at you. Tell the boys how you pushed me off the ladder Danny, and came at me with your zipper down. Pleeeese release me let me gooooo..."

"I didn't push you. I didn't. You fell when I grabbed your..." Danny fell back against the wall, defeated at last.

There was a feeling of collective surprise when he admitted what he had done. They all knew it but hearing him say it was unexpected. I felt victorious.

I turned and passed Smitty the screw gun. "He's all yours now." Then I turned to Ed. "All right with you if I go back to work with Robby after I get my hand cleaned and wrapped in the shack?"

Smitty unscrewed Danny, and held him to the wall while I packed up my tools. I was content but Danny was consumed by rage. Smitty continued, "The Hall is going to have to hear about this. You can wait for your check or we'll mail it to ya. I'm sorry Danny, but this is it."

Danny got angry. "It's all her fault! Because of her I'm losing my job. Mother FUCKING cunt! You gonna lay her off too?

I was so freaked out I was pacing. "Tell me Danny, do you eat with that mouth? And all that whining?" I tsked. "It just makes you look like an emotionally impotent twit."

"Hey, hey, hey, sister. Language." Smitty shook his head and paternally took me by the elbow to lead me away from Danny. "As your shop steward I gotta tell ya; you can't go around screwing people to walls."

I was too shaken from the assault to address the double standard around language but had to laugh. I knew that showing emotion would be used against me so I spoke quickly to cover how I felt. "Well, you kept telling me you couldn't do anything until someone hurt me." I held up my hand to his eye level and flashed my bloody palm in front of him. "Well. He hurt me."

"But he's gonna lose his job," Smitty replied defiantly.

"I still don't care. He screwed himself. I just shined the light on him like a good little helper." It infuriated me that I had to defend myself for defending myself. I also knew what happened to women who reported sexual harassment, especially a lesbian on a construction site in the 1980s. And there was the underlying fear of exposing intimate physical details that always made me weigh my choices carefully.

"Well now I have to let him go. You just don't know the trouble you've started." Smitty turned and walked away.

The trouble I started? I couldn't believe I was being blamed for this as I walked slowly along the dimly lit corridor. I was alone and keenly aware of the power my co-workers had over me as men, the power my secret had to silence me; and how much perpetrators rely on our silence. The tangible threat of sexual assault was foremost in my mind but the idea that I was causing any kind of trouble for Danny, because I wouldn't let him rape me, was completely outrageous. I wanted to vomit again. With only twenty minutes left in the day, I meandered through the building and exited out the back.

A New Twist

Soon after screwing Danny to the wall I got transferred to a different job. I wasn't surprised and welcomed the change from concrete and sheetrock to restoring an 1860's era building. A number of renovations had been made over the years and we were there to undo all that. It was nice working in a renovation environment rather than an industrial one. Finish jobs are hard to come by and I was feeling lucky to be there. I was also a little suspicious about this transfer but didn't want to jeopardize it. "Time for you to get your chance at some finish work," Smitty said when he handed me my last check and the address for my new job.

This was a new scene altogether. The crews were smaller and more racially diverse. There was one other woman, Sheila, who was a laborer. She was assigned to work with the sandblasters who were cleaning the paint off the marble columns and carved moldings. The areas being blasted were closed off but the sand could not be contained. And that was where my career ended. I wrenched my back slipping on sand while picking up my tools. In a split-second my world changed forever.

My employers insurance denied my workers comp claim. I spent six months on bedrest, which gave me time to coordinate doctors and lawyers to get my claim started. My possibilities would be determined by the outcome of a court appeal. Finally the day came. The elevator left me off on the sixth floor and I followed the arrows to the Accident Board. I stood in the doorway and looked at the other people waiting there; injuries of every misfortune. It really struck me when I sat down with them. Someone called my name. I rose, painfully. I hadn't had a paycheck in six months, medical bills were piling up and the union's lawyer never returned my calls. Suddenly I had to trust him with my future and I felt like a fool.

I followed him down a hallway with small cubicles on each side. He escorted me into one and we discussed my case for twenty minutes. Never once did he ask what I wanted but he had presented a plan on my behalf. These months of misery seemed so trite just then. He was nervous, and kept telling me to relax; the way insecure people with no self-awareness often do.

After we talked we returned to the waiting room. My case was scheduled in his name because, well, that's just how things are. The insurance company's Dr. had not sent us a copy of their medical report so we had no idea what to expect. Our only other option was to reschedule, which would take months while they continued to withhold my worker's compensation payments. They were playing the waiting game.

An officer from the court stepped into the hall and called a few cases into the courtroom. We followed along with the others and heard the judgments of the cases before mine. I was scared, but subtly confident too. Who in their right mind could look at me bent and hunched over, then send me back to work in construction? My lawyer ventured to the judge's bench. Another three-piece suit rushed in, slapped a folder on the table and passed another to the judge. The judge read through my file in less than a minute; issued the Order of Payment to include workers compensation, physical rehab and re-employment services. It took me longer to sit down than it did to determine my future. The lawyers chatted to each other and then joined me in the hallway. I turned to mine and asked, "So, that's it?"

"Yup."

It took about a week to get that all in writing. I got my retroactive workers' comp payments, they approved my medical expenses and paid them in full; and now I was off to rehab.

* * * * * *

"The doctor will see you now. This way please."

I hated this woman. For a year and a half the insurance company's doctor had stated that my injury did not interfere with my ability to work construction, although it was required that I attend their rehab program before returning to work. I attended the Work Hardening program every day for eight months. My six-hour day consisted of physical therapy exercises, occupational therapy and weight training. I joined thirty-five other workers recovering from occupational injuries. We were all required to attend this rehab program sponsored by the workers comp insurance company. They were paying themselves for our rehab. I met with their doctor weekly.

She was more interested in why I didn't shave my legs than she was in my damaged discs.

"Okay." The doctor greeted me as she sat down on her ugly green chair and made notes in my file. "Over here now. Bend to the right as far as you can. More. Is that it?"

"Yes." I straightened up.

"Now bend to the left. As far as you can. Un-huh. Bend forward now. All the way. Ok, good. Now bend back toward me."

"I don't do that."

"What do you mean you don't do that? Just do it." She demanded.

I put my hands on my lower back and tried to bend backwards. Tears welled in my eyes. "I can't do it!"

She made some more notes, shut the file folder, and placed it on the examining table. "How's it going in Occupational Therapy?"

"Okay I guess."

"How much can you carry now?"

"I'm up to sixteen pounds."

"That's more than last month. You carry that for fifteen minutes?"

"No. Only seven. I stop when it hurts," I stated.

"Hurts how?" She challenged me.

"Across my lower back and down my leg." I showed her where the pain started, and traveled down my leg.

"Your test results don't show any nerve damage. You can't have pain down your leg. You have to try harder."

"I'm doing the best I can!" I felt the shame that all bullies hope to impose on vulnerable people.

"Twelve pounds was your best last month. Now you can carry sixteen pounds. So it hurts a little. It's going to hurt until you get better."

Feeling defeated, all I could do was repeat my last remark more firmly. "I'm doing the best I can." I knew that I was and that she didn't care. It was demoralizing to be so physically limited; a real threat to my self-esteem.

"You can get dressed now. Schedule your next appointment on your way out." The door shut quietly behind her.

I scheduled my next appointment and went to Occupational Therapy. My OT routine totaled an hour and forty-five minutes, broken into ten or fifteen-minute workouts. I liked OT and Louisa, my occupational therapist, most of all. This was the only part of my six-hour day that gave me any insight on my actual limits and abilities. Even though I mistrusted the motive and the environment, I trusted her.

Half way through my OT session Louisa came by to check in with me. She stepped in alongside me and slowed to match my pace. "Shoulders back. Keep your knees bent. How was your visit with the doctor this morning?"

"I'll be the last to know." I rested my crate of weights on the shelf.

She smiled again. "I'm due to make my evaluation soon. How's your pain?"

"I want to go home."

"You can at 4:30." She smiled.

"I can't keep doing this." I rebutted.

58

"Hang in there. Would you like to see the vocational specialist?"

I picked up my crate and the two of us walked to the other side of the room. "Is that my ticket out of here?"

"Off the record, it mostly depends on my judgment of what you can and cannot do...I think you know what I mean. What do you want to do?"

I thought a minute. "Yea, I'd like to talk with the Vocational Counselor."

"The Voc Counselor's job is to try to get you employed. If nothing works out, they may just have to retrain you." She smiled knowing full well that retraining was my goal. The only reason I kept coming to the program every day was to prove to the insurance company that physical labor was no longer an option for me. Work Hardening was the price I had to pay. If I could endure being a cash cow for the insurance company I would get retraining.

Ending my career in the trades took me to a dark place. There was a familiar sadness to physical failure and I was starting to wonder if they were connected. I had to focus on getting out of there. It was a lot of work, more emotional than physical; and degrading to know that I needed to fail to be approved for retraining. All that time alone with my body gave me reason for pause. Sometimes we need a big pause to ease ourselves through major changes. My body was telling me something but I didn't know what, or maybe I just didn't want to.

"I can't evaluate you until Thursday afternoon. I'll have my report in by Friday. Check in with the front desk for an appointment with Wesley early next week. We have to see what he comes up with for career possibilities before I can alter your routines in here." She spoke respectfully and directly while keeping a watchful eye out on her other patients.

We were interrupted by a yell from across the room. "Hey, Louisa. Over here." We both turned. Ralph was peddling a stationary bicycle with one leg. His foot slipped off the pedal and he needed her help.

"I'll be right there." She started towards Ralph, but turned back to me and smiled. "Hang in there. You're on the way out." It was closing in on 4:00. I finished up early and took the subway home.

I Don't Think So

"So Miss; ahhh, Ms, um. Hi, I'm Wesley, the Vocational Counselor for this facility. Let's get settled in my office and see what I can do for you." He offered me a limp handshake.

I followed him down the familiar hallway, past the exam rooms and the prosthesis fitting room to the last door on the right. I waited for him to enter.

He motioned toward the chair. "Please, make yourself comfortable will you?"

"Ha!" I laughed. "I have been trying to do that for the last two and a half years."

"I see here that you've worked as a carpenter for fifteen years. That's very impressive. You don't look old enough to have done manual labor for that long. Do you think you'll be able to continue with that line of work?"

"My doctors advise me against it. My body concurs."

"I see. Well what was your major in college?"

"College? I majored in Sociology and Journalism before I got kicked out." I held my hands up in front of him. "These are my credentials."

Wesley glared at my hands over his stylish glasses. "I can see I have my work cut out for me. How about a resume?"

I just smiled and showed him my hands again. He glared over his glasses. "What kind of work would you like to do if you had a choice?"

I sat there. Even with all the talk about retraining, I'd never given it a chance to sink in. "I really don't know. It would probably make sense to get some computer training."

"Well, my goal here is to get you back to work as quickly as possible. What about transferable skills?"

"What do you mean?"

"Oh you know. Like, how about office work, receptionist or secretarial?" Can you teach? Ever been a Waitress?"

I laughed out loud. "I can read blueprints. I've supervised crews of painters and carpenters."

That was not what he wanted to hear. "Have you done any other type of work? You know, more suitable for someone such as yourself?" Do you have hobbies that could lead you into a career? Things like that."

"Hhmmmmmm." I thought about it. "I have no other training. I think I need to shy away from physical work. I am good with plants."

"Ah plant maintenance. Now there's a growing field." When I didn't laugh he caressed his necktie and continued. "Okay let's do this. I have a test here that should give us an idea of your interests and strengths. It takes about forty-five minutes. I'll go down the hall and make some phone calls while you take the test. Then we'll have an idea where to start." He placed the test booklet on the desk in front of me, set a timer and left the room quietly.

Wesley returned and stood in the doorway until the timer went off. I put down my pencil. "Let's see what we have here. I made some progress which we'll get to in a minute." He ripped open the answer sheet and skimmed the results. "Very impressive. This is good." He then put my test sheet in my file and told me about the phone calls he had made.

"I looked into plant maintenance jobs. Let me talk this over with the folks in OT so they can work on a routine to fit your new job description. The most you'll have to lift is fifty pounds, but with a hand truck so that's really nothing. Let's meet Tuesday after next and firm this up."

I was dumbstruck. This man just determined my future like it was his. "Yea, unhuh. Am I done here?" I rose slowly, turned and closed the door behind me. I couldn't shake the feeling that I was being swept out to sea for the first wave to carry off. The plan came together so fast that I couldn't trust it... There had to be more that I didn't know... I was being pushed into something without enough information. It ripped the band-aid off a familiar feeling of vulnerability that had been covered for decades. That wound had not begun to heal but it did teach me to trust my own instincts. I decided to make some calls of my own before my next meeting with Wesley. There's no harm in taking chances when you've got nothing to lose.

I woke early to get my paperwork in order on the day I was meeting with Wesley. I was still trying to decide if I was asleep and having a nightmare, or awake in my real life. I was in a lot of pain, depressed, and tired of being tired. I appreciated having a routine but my recovery had reached a plateau. Rehab did nothing for me at this point.

Louisa remained supportive of my goals while I pushed hand trucks, carts, and jugs of water in Occupational Therapy. I worked really hard but could only do a task for ten or twelve minutes. We questioned the plant maintenance company when they came to the rehab office. Louisa quickly confirmed that plant maintenance would never work for me. I tried hard to see these failures, each humbling one of them, as another step closer to my goal. It was an obscene waste of time, emotional stamina, and staff hours. It was hard to accept that getting approved for training meant proving to the insurance company that I couldn't do the things I knew I couldn't do. The time I'd wasted could have launched me in a new career. But someone somewhere valued my recovery differently. All my dealings with rehab involved listening to professionals talk the talk of patient care, while the cost of my rehab lined their pockets. I kept returning to the fact that I'd mastered a trade after fifteen years, ran my own business for ten years but did not qualify for minimum wage jobs. Being a pawn in this game had to end. I knew they wanted me to give up but they had no idea how much patience I could muster.

I sat in the lobby by the front door and waited for my appointment with Wesley. "Right this way, Jean. Sorry to keep you waiting."

"Beats pumping iron," I replied as I followed him down the corridor for what I hoped was the very last time. I followed him into his little beige room with no windows, paused and sat when prompted.

"So how's the job search going?" He asked while shuffling papers to find my file.

"I think the job search is over," I replied calmly.

"You found a job? That's great. Tell me about it." He was still shuffling files and did not look up at me.

"Found a job? No." I handed him a pile of job rejections. "I'm done with this job search. All you're doing at this point is paying yourselves to keep me here. I'll save you the trouble of reading through all that. I've gotten turned down for thirteen jobs since I saw you two weeks ago. I'm thirty-five years old. I made a good union rate before I got hurt and now I'm not fit to operate a copy machine. If you can't see your way clear to recommend me for retraining than you're off your fucking nut!" It wasn't exactly the speech I had prepared, but it did get his attention. I didn't realize how much my voice had risen until someone reached in from the hallway and shut the door.

He finally looked at me, mouth agape.

"Well?" I leaned forward just a little.

He caressed his necktie and cleared his throat. "Well, um, what were you thinking you'd like to do?" He finally asked.

"This is the computer age. I want to give that a shot."

He stared at me as if I weren't there. "Okay. You know what? There are these federally funded programs for women just like you, women trying to get back in the workforce." He was sliding drawers open and closed. "I have the forms here somewhere."

"What or who are women just like me? Disabled construction workers? That sounds a little obscure for federal funding."

"Here's the application. Take a look." He reached across the desk and handed me the six-page application.

I looked it over. "Number of dependents? Child support amount? Are you receiving food stamps?" I dropped the application on the desk. "I don't think so. This is for welfare mothers. I'm not on welfare."

He stiffened and looked down at me from his overly-padded office chair. In a condescending voice he said, "This is no time for pride, Jean. I know it's hard, but you can't afford pride at this stage of your life. If you want funding for retraining you're going to have to give this a shot."

I pushed myself all the way back in my chair, took a deep breath and paused before I could reply.

"No, I can't afford to be proud. But you can afford to retrain me. How can you sit there and suggest that I take funding away from Welfare mothers? That money is for people who have nothing. I know there's money allotted for retraining. I have been a very patient, patient for the last nine months. I have been rejected until it hurts. I'm not doing this anymore."

"But these things take time. There are some Community Colleges and Adult Ed courses you might want to check out first.

Out came my folder. "As a matter of fact I already have." I handed him a brochure from the school of my choice. "I've already toured the school and passed the exam. The application fee has been paid. Here's the receipt so you can reimburse me. Courses start in three weeks. The director of admissions tells me that there should be no problem getting approval for the next semester. Apparently, they work with you and this program all the time. Roger sends his best, by the way."

"But..." He took his glasses off, caressed his tie and used it to wipe his glasses. "We have to go through OT. There's probably a typing requirement. And then the Department of Rehabilitation has to approve it. This will take six weeks at least. You can't just take care of this on your own."

I explained each letter as I handed them over. "Here's a letter from my doctor. Here's the report from OT and Louisa's recommendation. My typing is up to fifty-two words per minute, and the Department of Rehab has approved this already. They also want to know why this is coming from ME and not YOU. It's all in their letter. The only thing standing in my way now is you." I smiled.

"You have to be discharged by our doctor before we can proceed. It will take at least a week to make that appointment..."

"I'm seeing her when I leave here." I cut him off as I slowly rose from my chair.

Wesley started sliding drawers open and closed again. "I can see you've done your homework."

I handed him the retraining form that I had already filled out. "All it needs is your signature. I don't want to keep the good doctor waiting."

Wesley stalled and stammered. He looked the form over twice. He signed it below my signature and slid it across the desk without looking at me. "I'm glad we found something you'll be...." When he finally looked up I was gone.

I went back to the waiting area to wait for my next appointment.

"The doctor will see you now."

I looked up and saw the nurse, Tamika, smiling. She led me down the hallway as she had many times before. "You know the routine. There's a gown on the table."

I put on my gown and shivered in the tiny air conditioned room.

The doctor entered and asked, "How are you doing?" As usual, she spoke without looking at me.

"It's a bit nippy in here," I shivered.

"Maybe you need more exercise to get your blood circulating."

"Maybe I need my clothes," I countered.

"Didn't I just see you? What brings you in today?"

"I'm here to be discharged."

"Oh you've got a while before I can discharge you."

"Yea, well, I have my retraining orders here and I start school in three weeks. I need to be discharged." I felt empowered telling a doctor what I wanted for a change.

"You can't do that yet. You're not ready."

"The department of Rehab thinks I'm long overdue. They are very curious to know why you're keeping me here.

"I see. Well let's take a look at you then. Walk heal-to-toe across the room."

I followed her commands to bend this way and that.

"You can get dressed now. I think we've done all we can for you here. I'm discharging you."

Even though I knew that was coming, I was stunned to hear her say those words. The contradiction was screaming to be noticed. "Eighteen months ago, when my body was twisted like a pretzel, you said there was nothing wrong with me. Then when my lawyer got me into your Work Hardening program you said I needed nine months of physical and occupational therapy. Now that the Division of Rehab has approved my retraining I'm suddenly free to go? Isn't the insurance industry marvelous?"

She left the room without a word. Tamika waited until she left and gave me a big hug. "Get a copy of your medical records before you leave. Good luck." She departed behind the same door.

I dressed as quickly as I could. My delight hadn't totally settled in but I could feel the smile spreading across my face. I got my discharge papers from Anita at the front desk and smiled even more.

Anita leaned across the desk and whispered. "I thought they'd never let you out of here." They liked you because you live here. You were money in their pockets without travel and hotel expenses."

I agreed. "They put the guys up in hotels and cover their meals and travel. All I got was subway fare. They wouldn't pay for childcare until I brought my two year old in and let him loose in PT." We both laughed at the memory of how quickly they came up with the money to avoid that liability. "Can I have a copy of my medical records, please? I don't mind waiting."

"Sign right here." Anita had already copied my file. She handed me an extra-large folder with a grin.

"Thanks, Anita. I am soooooo Out. Of. Here."

After spending nine excruciating months in rehab to get this far, I was also feeling sad about meeting my goal. Being granted approval for retraining meant the end to the work I dearly loved. Starting over in a new career would be hard enough, but there was an emotional toll to this loss that I couldn't bear to accept at the time.

I was feeling completely alone and it made me sad to acknowledge how familiar that felt. Somewhere in my past I had learned that I was on my own. Needing help from others took too much explaining. I used the physical power of labor and sports to make up for the ways my body failed and that validation was slipping away. Now my body was calling me to catch up, forcing me to pay attention; to look at the emotional traumas I had endured as well as the physical ones. Now my body was forcing me to stop and pay attention to things I didn't want to know. It was much easier to deal with an occupational injury than a medical anomaly that had no name. I needed to make peace with my trauma and not just recover from an injury. This might just be a time for me to heal.

I pulled myself back to the present and looked for the people I wanted to see before leaving. Louisa was on the top of that list. I found her working lotion on the stump of Emmanuel's arm. "I've been liberated," I said smiling.

"Where to from here?" she asked, unable to look up.

"Computer school starts in three weeks."

She stopped, excused herself from Emmanuel and gave me a hug. "That's great. I'm happy for you. You worked really hard and I'm glad you got your break."

"I really appreciate everything you did for me while I was here." The moment reminded me of my union partners and, as with most of them, I didn't want to see anyone in this building ever again. Ever. I wished the others well and walked out for the very last time.

Starting Over

Starting over is scary but uncertainty can be rich with opportunity. I walked across the street to the mall and sat on a marble bench. I looked around the building with the appreciation of someone who knew what was behind those walls, which I did since I built a lot of them. Working in the trades was my life until suddenly it wasn't. Being granted retraining took the edge off the bitter fact that I had to start over in a new career.

This wasn't new to me. The first time I had to start over changed my life even more than losing my career to disability. When I was thirteen I got sent home from camp with abdominal pain. My doctor discovered an imperforate hymen preventing the flow of menstrual blood. I was scheduled for a simple surgery to open my hymen so menses could flow. But the surgery revealed I had no vagina, just a dimple, and they couldn't find a uterus. I had typical female sex traits, body hair and breasts, so they guessed I had ovaries but they didn't know where. I was sent to specialists in Philadelphia for a series of diagnostic tests. Their narrow definition of normal threw me to the margins. I thought I was a girl but everyone told me I needed surgery to become a woman. I was too young to ask questions, or to slow the process down to match my own state of mind. I had major doubts about what was going on, and what was being done to me. Frightened in an oversized hospital gown I did what I was told. I was diagnosed with *congenital absence of vagina*

72

and *sexual dysfunction.* I was suddenly and shamefully different. I received sympathy and even pity for the loss of fertility, but the most pressing concern was to get me a vagina. ASAP. The pain that started this process was ignored. I went from selling Girl Scout Cookies to correcting my *sexual dysfunction* in one afternoon.

The doctors talked to my parents about vaginal reconstruction so I could have a "normal sex life with my husband when I got married". What husband? And why couldn't he adjust as he would for any other physical concern? My parents took me down the only path available at the time, the path of corrective surgery. There were no words for this so my mom called it, Your Little Problem. She wasn't disparaging me; there just wasn't much else to say. I was told I'd be safer to keep this to myself so My Little Problem became a very big secret and changed my life in a very big way. Having my sex and gender challenged during puberty actually neutered my soul. Learning I could never have kids forced me to reinvent my future. I had a lot of my own questions that no one wanted to answer. I couldn't decide who was more upset about my body. Was it me, or the people treating me? My Little Problem became the elephant in the room but I was the only one who could see it.

So here I was again, starting over and feeling adrift about my future. Once again I found myself in a position of limited support that I had to make stronger by my own survival. My body, already vulnerable and compromised, was telling me it had had enough. I felt overwhelmed by physical challenges I didn't want to think about. I strolled through the mall feeling melancholy, as though I was saying good-bye to old friends. I remembered all the characters I had met while I was there, and how much more I had learned about social constructs than industrial construction. Robby and I experienced the same resentment of white men even though we were resented for different reasons. Class was revealed by an electrician whose elitism outranked sisterhood when she belittled me for being a carpenter. "Carpenters are just laborers with tools. Anyone can pound nails." Those small minds left an impact but they were not my problem anymore. I had my own insecurities to address.

Still feeling inspired by my retraining victory when I got home, I found an article my sister sent me years ago. I was afraid to read it at the time but I knew not to throw it away. I sat in my recliner and read it all the way through. I was stunned. I read it again. And again. Four paragraphs of medical jargon described a syndrome known since the early 1800s as Mayer-Rokitansky-Kuster-Hauser syndrome. It connected all my physical challenges: my back problems, infertility and hearing loss. And it occurs in one out of 4500/5000 women! The connection this syndrome made to my back and hearing problems made me numb. Why did I not know this? In all the time I spent with doctors, why did none of them think to mention an actual diagnosis? Could I have avoided years of disability had I known I was predisposed to back problems because of MRKH? Could I have avoided hearing aids had I known that hearing loss was related to my diagnosis? These are things I will never know but

74

always have to live with. Why was my younger sister the only one to give it a name? Anxious to learn everything I could I requested my hospital records for the testing and surgeries I endured in my teens. Learning there was a syndrome helped me feel like a person who was different rather than an android who had been assembled with spare parts. I had a few weeks before computer school and spent them in a medical library. I copied every article about MRKH, reproduction and sexual development that I could find. What I was learning made it painfully clear that this wasn't just about bodies. A whole new perspective was growing from very old emotions. Information peeled layers off my medical secret to expose a person feeling confused and hungry to know more. How do I monitor the health of my ovaries? How many ovaries do I have and where the hell are they? How will I experience menopause? What about pap smears? I now had a chance to start over with My Little Problem too. I wasn't sure I could bear it but I couldn't turn back now.

Assaultra-Sound

I focused on school for the next six months and tried t find a gynecologist. I would call for an appointment and get demoralized by the standard questions. "Are you pregnant? When was your last period?" I also had my ow reservations and fears. I didn't know how to talk to friend: for guidance or support because there was so much I just didn't know. I made an appointment with my primary car provider hoping to get a referral through her.

"Good afternoon. Nice to see you today. Tell me mor about this referral you're asking for."

I took a seat. "Well, Doc, I think the abdominal pain I've been having is related to my reproductive anomaly. They never found my ovaries when I was a kid. Now that I'm getting older I want to know if I have both of them an how to monitor them. There's a lot of cancer in my family and I'd like to stay ahead of it. Have you heard of MRKH Mayer-Rokitansky-Kuster-Hauser syndrome?"

"No, I don't believe I have. Does this have anything to do with your missing vagina?"

Damn! She had to say that. People could sympathize with infertility but being born without a vagina is what made MRKH seem so freaky. I felt my body withdraw. "I think it has something to do with the pain that no one has been able to figure out. I think I'm having menstrual cramps but, that seems odd since I don't have a uterus, right?

"Did you ever have an ultrasound to look for your ovaries or anything?" She asked as she washed her hands.

"No. My intervention took place before that technology."

"OK, then. I want you to get an ultrasound so we can get a look at everything. OK?"

"There's definitely something going on so the sooner the better." I was both excited and afraid of what they might find.

She poked around my abdomen. "Is there any regularity to your pain? Any other symptoms?

"Yes. It feels like a cramp, sort of tightening and it's always in the same place. And I've tracked it. The pain is monthly." I knew this because the timing was similar to my wife's menstrual cycle.

"Interesting. Well, you do have typical sex characteristics so you have at least one ovary that produces estrogen." She poked around some more then ordered an ultrasound for the following week. I welcomed the idea of being proactive.

"Thanks, Doc." I'm sure she could hear the trepidation in my voice.

"We'll get to the bottom of this. I'll tell them not to do an internal pelvic scan. You'll need a full bladder for an abdominal ultrasound. Drink as much water as you can an hour before your appointment. And I'll set you up with a gynecologist as soon as possible. Ok?"

My brain went numb so I just nodded. I was trying not to panic. The medical madness that followed my hymen surgery at thirteen was a nightmare I didn't want to experience again. I spent a lot of time having tests done to confirm my sex and being probed by curious doctors and interns with multiple instruments in multiple holes at multiple times. My chromosomes were counted and discussed in front of me as if they couldn't be true. "We should run that test again. Just look at her." They examined every inch of my pubescent sex anatomy with a disapproving lens and my relationship with my body ended. There was so much focus on the woman I should be that I lost all knowledge of the girl that I was. Everyone wanted to fix me so I must have been terribly wrong. But that was then. I was hoping this round of testing would be different. It just had to be.

I didn't want to travel on a full bladder for my ultrasound so I arrived early enough to drink water there. I hated this with every ounce of my being yet I knew I had to take control any way that I could. I got off the bus and walked a few blocks along the river to the medical building. Three deep and calming breaths and in I went. I got off the elevator and walked down the sterile white hallway to check in for my test.

"Good morning. I'm Jean. I'm here for an ultrasound at 10:30. I came early to fill my bladder here."

"Have a seat and we'll call you when the doctor is ready." The receptionist looked up from her computer. "Oh, Jean. You don't need a full bladder for the pelvic ultrasound."

Here we go. I was already stressed-out so I tried to find the easiest way to explain this without falling apart. "My doctor instructed me to fill my bladder for this test. It has to be done abdominally."

Not wanting to be challenged she replied. "Your doctor was wrong to tell you to fill you bladder for a pelvic ultrasound."

I leaned into her window to avoid sharing details about my anatomy with the entire waiting room. "It can't be done the typical way. It has to be done abdominally. I'm not having a pelvic ultrasound."

Again she assumed she knew more about me than I did. "Since you're here to check your ovaries, you're having a pelvic ultrasound."

I took a deep breath. "That's just not possible."

The receptionist pushed her chair away from her desk and stood to declare. "Oh! You're the one without a vagina!"

I could feel my face burn with humiliation as all the people in the waiting room turned to stare at me. I wanted to leave but I knew I'd never come back so I found a seat in the corner to wait. I drank water, read magazines and internalized my shame. All I cared about was getting this over with as soon as possible. I was finally called from the waiting room and guided down another hallway.

I entered the examining room and put on the gown as instructed. A doctor came in, introduced himself and assured me this would be over quickly.

The ultrasound gel felt cold on my stomach. I watched the screen as he moved the probe from one side of my stomach to the other. "Are you sure you have ovaries? I don't see anything where they are supposed to be."

"Well that's kinda of why I'm here... to find them and make sure they're ok. And my pain is over here." I pointed to show him where to look.

"But your ovaries are supposed to be here." He arrogantly replied as he pressed down with the probe to assert his authority.

Again I pointed to the area where I felt pain. "I don't think we can assume anything is where it's supposed to be since I don't have most of what is supposed to be there, right? Something is causing a lot of pain. Here. What do you see here?"

"Well it can't be your ovaries but I'll take a look." He sighed with contempt, as though I was making this difficult For Him. He slid the probe over my stomach and pushed down hard. I peed a little but didn't care.

"Owww! That's the spot!" I looked over toward the screen but I couldn't determine one gray area from another. He tapped on the keyboard a few times to capture an image and wiped off my stomach.

"You can empty your bladder in there," he said as he pointed to a bathroom. "Then we'll continue the exam. I found your right ovary and there appears to be a cyst on it. It's small and probably benign. He rolled the cart to the foot of the exam table. When you hop back up we'll finish the exam."

"I thought we were done," I questioned.

"I think I can get a better view internally."

It took me a minute to realize he meant vaginally. "I doubt that very much. Did you read my chart? My vagina doesn't connect to the rest of my reproductive system."

Having to say that aloud distanced me from my body even more.

"I've done thousands of these. I'll get a better view this way. It will be ok." It might have been OK for him but I was the one being probed.

I was skeptical, but desperate to learn more so I talked myself into it. My providers have always focused on what I wasn't born with and never gave notice to the organs I do have. How could I exercise preventative care if I don't know what to care for? I settled into the stirrups for the next part of the exam.

Again with the cold gel, but this time on my labia. "How's that," he asked as he started to insert the probe.

"I don't think this is going to work, Doc. And you're hurting me."

"Just a minute now," he assured me. "It'll be ok," he said as he pushed harder.

"No, it's not ok." I clarified. "This isn't working. You're hurting me, Doc. Wait! STOP! NO-owww!"

The doctor wobbled backwards. I was horrified to see his bloody nose but I didn't regret the reflex to defend myself when he pushed harder after I told him to stop.

"You kicked me!" He indignantly exclaimed as he wiped the blood off his upper lip.

I pushed myself upright. I grabbed the sheet off the table, used it to wipe the ultrasound gel from my crotch and tossed it on the floor. I got dressed and walked out. Numb, and fueled by adrenalin I fled down the stairs from the sixth floor, into the lobby and out to the street. I was in shock. I didn't know where I was going until I reached the bus stop.

The assault of his authority was harder to process than his assault with the probe. I had no problem defending myself against a workmate but I submitted to an exam I knew wouldn't work because a doctor told me to. I was proud that I fought off Danny and Burt and elevator jerks but it took me years to admit that I had never, until then, been able to protect myself from white coat violence. I didn't know how to pursue it without exposing myself to ridicule. I was mad at myself for trusting an overly arrogant doctor more than I trusted myself. The shame victimized me even more. I was conditioned to believe it was my fault because my body didn't deserve their respect. I blocked the incident out for years and my body took it on. Noting the lie his report years later proved he knew he had crossed the line. "Internal exam, requested by patient, was unsuccessful."

Oh, The Irony

Later the following week I met with the gynecologist. He rose to greet me as I entered the room. "I apologize for not having a thorough look at your test results and previous records. Please, sit and help me get up to speed." He smiled and gestured toward a chair.

I liked his cordial approach. He was younger than me and shorter so I sat quickly. "Thanks. Where to begin? Are you familiar with MRKH?" He looked at me pleading for more. "Mayer-Rokitansky-Kuster-Hauser syndrome?"

"I'm familiar with Rokitansky, which explains your vaginal agenesis, but I don't know the rest of it."

Again my condition was defined by my vagina. "More men's names that define women's anatomy," I explained with a smile. The problem for me is a persistent pain. I suspect it's related to my reproductive issues." Every time I had to explain that to a doctor was more frustrating than the last.

"You were born without a uterus, right? There could be endometrium tissue or remnants that respond to your hormone cycle. Do you have ovaries?"

I clarified. "The ultrasound only found one, and it looks like it has a cyst so I'm concerned about that. I'd like to know if I have the other one and if it's ok. I don't know what menstrual cramps feel like any more than you do, but from what I've heard my pain feels like that."

"On a scale of one to ten?"

I hate that question. "Twelve."

"I see." I watched him restrain a smile, which endeared me to him. "Describe the pain. Frequency. Duration."

I paused for a moment of silence before I spoke. I had to separate my emotions from the facts. Past experience told me that fear and frustration had to be compartmentalized for doctors to take what I know seriously. "I get cramps for a few days and then they go away. Most of the time they're just noticeable but sometimes the pain is debilitating. The timing resembles a typical cycle, except...."

He cut me off. "Yes, this is interesting." He paused. "I'm sorry. Interesting for me usually means not so good for you. Anyway, I doubt you're actually menstruating but we really don't know what's going on in there. I can look laparoscopically and remove the cyst if it gets to the point where you can't stand it."

Grr. "I don't want another surgery but I really can't stand this so let's schedule the laparoscopy."

"I'd rather give it some more time. It might resolve itself."

"It's been over twenty years," I laughed. "It hasn't resolved itself by now and I don't think it will. It gets really bad. Sometimes I can't get out of bed."

"Let me know when you can't stand it and I'll schedule the procedure," he repeated.

He really wasn't getting it so I stood up and stepped toward his desk. "I can't stand it. There is a cycle to it. I'm pretty sure it's uterine and I need to know what's going on." I repeated firmly.

He looked up at me but didn't stand. Since he didn't believe it, it couldn't be true. A moment later he stood. "As I mentioned, I doubt it's serious."

I sat back down. "You can't know what it's not until you know what it is, right? Something is causing a lot of pain."

He nodded in agreement and smiled. "Okay. I'll have Sharon schedule it and we'll take care of this."

I rose to leave. "Thanks. I really appreciate it." I needed to assert my suspicions, "You're gonna find a uterus, I just know it." I said to tease him.

He didn't take the bait but replied with a kind smile.

Sharon called later that afternoon. I never dreamed I'd get this far and the range of emotions was exhausting. I was also struggling with chronic pain from my injury and job hunting in a new career. I withdrew; feeling like an observer in my own life... that I wasn't really experiencing this; just watching it happen. Watching it happen to me.

I passed the time on internet while I waited for my laparoscopy appointment. I discovered listservs that I never knew existed. I had been denied their support since I didn't have a diagnosis. I connected with other women who had also been told they were the only ones. I found people with many other variations of sex development and an even bigger Intersex community. I was comforted to learn that there were so many people who aren't considered normal, but I didn't want to be one of them. I wanted to separate myself...to think I was not like them because I have *normal* female chromosomes and that makes me a woman. At the same time, my *normal* female

85

chromosomes didn't protect me from the judgment, the dysphoria or the treatment that punished my MRKH body.

It had been a long time since I had been in a surgical setting and a lot was running through my mind. I didn't know what to think or how to feel. Attitudes about women's health had changed since the early 1970's, yet I felt like living proof that bias and ignorance were thriving. On laparoscopy day I checked in at the hospital and made my way to Pre-op. After they hooked me up to monitors, the anesthesiologist came in and hooked me up to a drip. He instructed me to count backwards as they wheeled me into the operating room. Ten Nine. Six. *Zzzzzzzzzzz.* Next thing I knew I was back where I started and very stoned.

"Oh good, you're awake." My doctor was standing by my side.

"What thyme is it?" I slurred through the anesthesia.

"Ten forty-five. You tolerated the procedure very well. Can you understand me?

"That didn't take wong. Did you fine my utrus? Remove da widdle trouble-bubble?"

He smiled self-consciously. "Actually, you have two." He paused to give that time to sink in. "I'm sorry to say I couldn't remove them laparoscopically. I did find your other ovary and it looks good. You have a hemi-uterus attached to each ovary and they appear to be healthy. I suspect your uterii are responding to your ovulation cycle and that is the cause of your pain. You can go home this afternoon and I'll see you in the office next week to discuss next steps. The good news is that everything looks healthy and there are no signs of cancer. The not so good news is that you need a hysterectomy, or technically, two. We can talk about it next time I see you. Get some rest."

I was not too groggy to comprehend next steps and shivered from the chill that gave me. I could feel my body sinking into a dark hollow. No sign of cancer is good but another surgery... Damn. The hymen surgery I had at thirteen didn't work so I had two more when I was fifteen. Those three surgeries didn't address my pain so I had this laparoscopy. Now the laparoscopy didn't work and I need two hysterectomies. Every time I think I'm getting closer to some answers I get more procedures and scars. Did my body parts suddenly appear or have they been there undetected all these years? Could my skin-graft vagina have been connected to a uterus enabling me to have children? I thought this was taken care of decades ago; so why are things acting up now? For years, doctors insisted that I didn't have a uterus and now I'm told I have two. All along I suspected my pain was uterine but my instincts just didn't count. I was glad to have that confirmed and furious what it took to find out. I was too groggy to make sense out of any of this. I just wanted to go home.

The Shift

A new light was dawning as I recovered from my back injury and exploratory laparoscopy at the same time. Learning they were related by a syndrome actually gave me a sense of wholeness. The work that came with my physical rehab helped me regain my confidence, which gave me emotional strength. All this information was swirling around in my head so I called the only other person who could appreciate the irony that I needed a hysterectomy, or two.

"Hi Ma. How's it going?

"Fine honey. How's your rehab coming along?"

"Still improving, thanks. And I'm getting used to the fact that my career as a carpenter is over. I'm still applying for computer jobs and looking forward to working indoors."

"Well that must be hard, but good for you."

"Thanks. So Ma, I have some interesting news. Are you sitting down?"

"What is it now?" She inquired cautiously.

"Well, I don't really know yet, but I'm going to the hospital for a hysterectomy next week. Well, actually two."

After a brief moment of silence she stammered. "But.. How can you... I don't understand. Are you alright?"

Aware that all the women in her family died of cancer was quick to reassure her. "Yes, so far. I'm still trying to resolve my abdominal pain. A cyst was found on my left ovary so I had a laparoscopy to take a look. We thought it would be a simple procedure to remove the cyst."

"Since when has Your Little Problem ever been simple?" We laughed, acknowledging the very private understanding we shared about my privates.

"Yea, I know, right. Well, I have a lot to tell you but first, I am pleased to report that there are no signs of cancer. The surgeon found my other ovary too, and it looks ok, but also has a cyst."

I could feel her sigh of relief from many miles away. "Well that's good to know. What brought all this on now?"

"I can't deal with the pain anymore. Rehab was distracting and I guess getting past it inspired me to look into this situation. Here's a fun fact for you. There's a name for My Little Problem. Libby sent me an article a while ago and I finally read it. Thing is, My Little Problem isn't just a one-off. I'm not a mistake. I have a medical condition; an actual syndrome." She made the usual sounds of acknowledgment so I continued.

"This syndrome includes all my physical challenges; my hearing problems, my back problems and my reproductive problems. And it has been documented since the early 1800s.

"Why do you kids need to know so much? Can't you just accept what's what and be happy with that?"

I laughed. "Well, Ma, I haven't known what to accept until now. I always felt like the Hunchback in the bell tower... horribly disfigured and misunderstood." I paused to take a breath and regroup. "So this syndrome is called Mayer-Rokitansky-Kuster-Hauser Syndrome."

"Hunh?"

"Fours men's names. My unique female sex anatomy is named after the four men who connected all these symptoms to a syndrome. It sure feels better to know I have a syndrome then to be told about all the things I don't have."

There was silence on the other end of the phone. I was worried. My mother could stop a train with her silence and I didn't want this conversation to end. We both needed it. I waited to give her some time but didn't want to lose the connection. I was pacing back and forth, hoping she would speak. "Ma, are you still there?" I heard her light a cigarette. "Yes. I guess I'm wondering why you're still thinking about this after all this time. We took care of it when you were younger... so you could get on with your life... not have to think about it anymore."

I was so stunned my knees buckled. I sat to gather my thoughts before I replied. I didn't want to yell at her but quickly explained, "Not a day goes by that I don't think about this. Every pregnant woman I see reminds me I can't have kids. Every tampon commercial reminds me I'm still waiting to become a real woman. I can't relate to my friends when they talk about their bodies, or go down the feminine products aisle without breaking into a sweat. The first time I bought pads for Ann I got six different kinds." I chuckled remembering the look on my wife's face when I brought them all home.

"Oh." Pause. Exhale. "I guess I never really thought about any of that. I'm a little miffed that no one told us there was a name for Your Little Problem. I guess that means you really aren't the only one." She was getting up to speed pretty quickly. "So there's a name for it?" I could feel her struggling with not knowing just as I had.

"Yup. And the incidence rate is one in five thousand so we're not uncommon, just unheard of. Here's another little secret we didn't know about. There are a lot of other physical variations that impact sex and reproductive development too... there are even support groups. All my specialists told me was that I would never meet anyone else like me, and that I needed surgery to have a normal sex life with my husband. Well, they got that wrong too."

"I don't want to talk about your hommm... homo... homosexual life. I love you and Ann but I don't want to know. I don't want to know about your brothers and their partners either, so don't get huffy."

We both laughed. "It's not about sex, Ma. It's about choice and losing ownership of my body. It's about..." I started to say it's about the difference between making love and rape but I stopped myself. "It's about being able to accept who I am now and who I was before all those surgeries. It's about having my sex and gender challenged and then confirmed like something OTHER people got to decide?" I really didn't want to harangue my mother for doing what she was told to do. She had limited support for this situation too. Her daughter's vagina wasn't a topic for bridge or theatre clubs. Dad wasn't really available and she had other kids at home. I paused.

91

"So one in five thousand," my mother pondered. "I guess that means this sort of thing just happens; it wasn't really my fault."

I never considered the guilt she must have carried. Gently I replied. "No Ma, it wasn't your fault. There are dozens of different variations for sexual development... like... one out of two thousand people are born with nonconforming sex anatomy! And I know you didn't take me to all those appointments and procedures to punish me for being different. We just didn't know. But they knew! They knew and didn't tell us! All I wanted to do was go water skiing, but Nooooooo, I had to spend my summer vacation getting a vagina for a fictitious husband! I didn't give three hoots about that, or about discussing intercourse with my parents in my early teens." We both laughed about that. Honestly, intercourse seemed like a colossal joke since I had discovered pleasure without a husband at a very young age.

We were both holding the silence and using it to feel closer to each other. Being raised Quaker makes silence a gift and I could feel her close in spirit from hundreds of miles away.

I was first to speak. "What are you thinking?"

"I was remembering the time you got so mad about the medical form for basketball camp."

"Oh yea, you said my periods were normal. After all I had been through. How could you forget your daughter would NEVER get a period? I didn't understand how you could call that normal?"

"Well, that was normal for you which was all they needed to know."

Her simple truth was so validating I was shaken by it. I loved and respected my mom more than I could ever express just then. Tears pooled in my eyes. Suddenly I was able to consider my physical history in terms of who I actually am and not who I was supposed to be. "Well, I guess you're right. I never thought of it that way before. There are so many people with atypical sex anatomy that we are more common than Down Syndrome and Cystic Fibrosis combined. We've all heard about those physical variations, but variations in sex development are kept a secret. We should be normalizing our existence, not our children's genitals without consent. I wish my providers spent half the time teaching me how to live with MRKH as they did trying to correct it." I felt a tirade coming on so I stopped talking.

Pause. Exhale. "Didn't you want your surgery?"

Hmmm. "Well nobody ever asked me what I wanted at the time and it's too late now. I felt more like a girl before all that went down than I do now, to be honest with you." I didn't want to burden my mom with my growing resentment; that I feel like a freak because of my surgeries not because of my vaginal dimple. Being born without a vagina was not my problem. Having to get one was the real problem. My heart started to sink so I changed the subject. "You know, Ma, I always wondered about the times we went to Philly for medical appointments but I never saw a doctor. Do you remember that?"

"Yes." Exhale. Pause. "It turned out that those appointments were for medical students to examine you. I didn't think they should be doing that to a thirteen or fourteen year old girl so we left."

I never considered how fiercely she worked to protect me. "We always went to Bookbinders, though." We laughed at those memories. Every time my mom took me out of school to go to Philadelphia for a doctor's appointment, she would take me to Bookbinders Restaurant for lunch. The treat was an unspoken reward that made me feel special. It happened enough to become a tradition. We had some awkward and hilarious conversations about sex, body parts and what was going to happen with the skin from my left butt cheek. At some point during the meal, we laughed so hard we cried. And then we would really cry but just a little; each being brave for the other. Tears said all there was to say. We had no words for the unknown reality that was becoming my life.

"We did the best we could by you." Her sigh sounded a little defeated.

"I know, Ma. I know. Since there were no words for this at the time, there was no way talk about it. Correction was the road they made us take. But they had the words and decided not to tell us. I thought you'd like to know this is something that just happens since nobody told us that. I've joined some support groups. The more I hear from other women the more I respect how you helped me with all of this. I'm sorry you had to do that and I want you to know I appreciate you for it."

"You were so sad. You seemed angry at the whole world. We didn't know how to help you and didn't really think anyone could."

"I think I was mad at the world because the world rejected me and made me an outcast. Learning there are so many other conditions like mine softens the loneliness a lot. I guess I took it out on the only person who was there for me and I'm sorry. In retrospect, I think therapy would have been a good idea," I suggested. "It might have made this easier for all of us."

"We considered that but I was afraid they'd have a field-day with you. It was never clear to me whether all the medical attention you were getting was for your benefit or theirs."

Hmmm. She really was two steps ahead of me. "That's a really good point. I guess I didn't know how much was going on behind the scenes. Thank you." More comforting silence.

I heard her exhale. "Your father and I thought we were being quite liberal for not waiting until you got married to schedule your surgery, I'll have you know." I could see her ornery smile from the tone of her voice. It was the early 70's after all.

"Well, you could have given me a little more notice when you did schedule it," I chuckled. I came home from school one day to learn I was having vaginal reconstructive surgery the next. Another secret to lie about that cut off any hope of support. "I would have skipped band practice and gone water skiing after school if I knew I'd miss graduation," I quipped.

"You had finals. We didn't want you to worry."

Another. Good. Point. Damn.

"Well honey, I hate to cut you short but I'm hosting bridge club tonight and need to get ready. Thanks for calling, I guess." We laughed and shared closing sentiments as we ended the call with a deeper level of respect for each other. This conversation with my mom was validating, and a tender reminder that my medical history will always be a part of me. The conversation also reminded me how much of my former self I had lost. Being celebrated as a medical success meant becoming someone I'm not, which made success a dubious value from that moment on.

I started to understand that being told I needed treatment is not the same as consent. I later learned that non-consensual genital surgeries are considered a form of torture.* These were facts I wasn't prepared to accept but my body somatized long ago. For decades I had been at odds with myself, accommodating normalcy and being who people wanted me to be. The child I was born was not allowed to mature and the death of her trapped me in a grief I couldn't grasp. I understood the loss, but I needed to acknowledge that feisty, innocent child; thank her for keeping me safe, and start letting her go.

I looked over at the large manila envelope on my desk. In it were the hospital records from my first three surgeries and some of the early diagnostic reports. I had yet to read them but felt their presence every time I walked by. I decided to take the plunge. I made a cup of tea and traveled back into time.

The summer I was fifteen, my family told people I would be on vacation as a cover story for getting my vagina. I missed family weddings and graduations for my McIndoe surgery. "...a slight dimple was present where the vagina was expected to be. A transverse incision was made. By means of sharp and blunt dissection a very adequate vagina was developed... a split thickness skin graft was obtained from the left buttocks and attached to the mold... The Balsa mold was then inserted into the cavity... The skin graft that extended was attached to the vaginal introitus... The vagina was closed... All sponges were accounted for." I don't know if I turned off my emotions to cope with the experience, or if emotions for this even existed at the time. This description of something meant to make me normal felt so artificial and surreal.

After my surgery I was sent to recover in the maternity ward. For seventeen days I shared a room with women having babies which emphasized my infertility. I had no visitors since I was 'on vacation' and no one knew to visit me. It was me and my mom, and a night nurse who would wake me in the morning sitting quietly by my bed. I later learned that she was protecting me from night shift intruders wanting to satisfy their curiosity as I slept.

Two weeks later I had the second phase of my McIndoe surgery, to have the mold and stitches removed. Then I was given vaginal dilators for postoperative therapy to keep my vagina functional. A functional vagina is defined as one that "will be able to accept a normal size penis". This intimate part of my body was defined in terms of someone else. The problem was solved, for everyone but me. I had two follow-up visits with my surgeon and the whole shebang was over. Even after three surgeries, there was no relief from my abdominal pain. Finally, all these years later a doctor was paying attention to what I cared about. I was hopeful that the upcoming hysterectomies would finally address what I needed. Lucky for me I was interesting...

* TORTURE: U.N. Committee Against Torture, General Comment No. 2, CAT/C/GC/2 (2007). - Report of the Special Rapporteur on violence against women, its causes and consequences, U.N. Doc. E/CN.4/2002/83 (2002).
   * Human Rights Watch: Date: 2017 "I Want to Be Like Nature Made Me." Medically unnecessary surgeries on intersex children in the US.

And Again

A month after my laparoscopy I returned to the hospital for my hysterectomies. Everything was the same as before. The anesthesiologist instructed me to count backwards as they wheeled me down the hall. Ten. Nine Seven. Six. Four. Zzzzzzzzzzz. Next thing I knew I was in the recovery room and very cold. A nurse brought me a blanket and asked how I was feeling. My doctor came over and told me how well I tolerated him again. "You'll have to spend the night to make sure everything is ok. You're going to be really sore for a few days. The left hemi-uterus was full of menses. The right one was smaller and the tissue was healthy. I had to peel them away so you could keep your ovaries. Everything looks good. Bed rest until I see you next week. I'll try to stop by before your discharge tomorrow. Take it easy. You've been through a lot." And he was off. I dozed off and on throughout the night and was discharged the next morning.

I was emotionally and physically depleted. Bedrest was a godsend. With so many recoveries in my past I was prepared to be laid up for a while. I had embroidery projects and doll house furniture kits to keep me entertained. And I still had some articles from the medical library. Reading them was hard after being kept in the dark for so long. I was overwhelmed by the measures medicine had developed to create vaginas, and furious that my MRKH care was limited to that.

99

The skin-graft surgery I had was the most common procedure at that time. Bowel and intestine are also used to make vaginas. I read one case where a vagina was transplanted from the patient's mother. My mother's used vagina? Creating a vagina by means of dilation is less invasive and the woman can control the process. The basic method is to apply enough pressure with different sized dilators to indent your tissue deep enough for an erect penis. It takes anywhere from two to eighteen months depending on how often you do it. Another procedure involves a device that dilates for you. A mold at your vaginal dimple is connected to the device that is attached to your stomach. Over the course of a week the tension is gradually increased to pull your vaginal dimple in enough to form a vagina. No matter which procedure or treatment you have, you might have to use dilators to keep your vagina from shrinking if you don't have frequent intercourse. I stopped using my dilators after the first few years. It was painful even after surgery, and felt emotionally self-defeating to continue. So I gave them names and hid them in the attic.

Reading the medical perspective about vaginal treatment was enlightening, but not nearly as helpful as what I was learning from MRKH and Intersex listservs. The case studies I had been reading about were no longer anonymous. They became real people with traumatic experiences, and I came to realize that their trauma was also mine. These people taught me more about bodies and courage in a week than any stack of articles or doctor ever could. Our dysfunction had been treated. Our success rates had been tallied. Then we are sent out on our own to make peace with it all. I felt driven to explore the impact of this so I asked some questions of my own.

My new career in public health data management gave me the skills needed to develop a survey. The data I collected from MRKH groups made me realize that this experience could not be captured in a questionnaire. We each have our personal experience with this and cope as best we can. I got most of my information from the question: "What Else Would You Like To Say?" There is so much more to MRKH than *normal sexual function*, so much more to the experiences I am hearing about now.

Every woman who answered my survey wished their doctors were better informed. Only four of their doctors had heard of MRKH before the initial pelvic exam. Two of those four hardly knew anything. The rest of our doctors were "shocked" or "excited" about treating us. One teen's doctor "ran into his office to look a few things up," and left her alone in the stirrups. Other women were referred to specialists without explanation. Most of us never knew we had a syndrome until years after our vaginal procedures.

All the women felt that the lack of gendered body parts threatened their identities, and for some it scars the most. We start living our lives as typical little girls. Then arbitrary judgments tell us we're not. Our identities crumble when we don't measure up. We are literally molded to fit social values. We are faced with questions about our most vulnerable selves during our most formative years. But how can you follow your heart to the answer when the process has ripped out your heart?

The women in the groups were passionate about helping other women, and for the need to sensitize doctors. One woman's doctor showed her a vaginal dilator and compared it to a shoe stretcher. He then told her she could become a nun. Another young girl was dehumanized when her doctor told her, "Some species respond to overpopulation by producing sterile females." Some doctors ask only about the sexual pleasure of male partners with no regard to their own patient.

In response to treatment, twelve of the fifteen who completed treatment felt it was required to be sexually active, normal or loved. The rest of the women felt that a vagina would complete them. Some women question the importance of vaginal intercourse. "What's the point? I'll never get pregnant... We share pleasure in many other ways."

Of the women with medical procedures; all were told by their doctors that their procedures were successful but not all of those women agreed. One woman had two surgeries before being happy with the result. Two women tried different procedures before getting a result they could live with. Vaginal penetration was too painful for some women or not possible at all. Only three of the twenty-one women were aware of sexual practices other than vaginal intercourse. A lot of women worried that their vaginas would not feel normal to their sex partners but most of the partners didn't notice. Yet one woman was called a "freak", one woman was asked why her vagina was "so shallow" and another woman was bluntly asked, "Can't you fix that thing?" Until that moment she thought she had.

There were far less studies about the psychosocial development of women born with vaginal agenesis. The doctors reported that their treatment made us normal. One article boasted how, "an angry, withdrawn, muscular girl was transformed into a woman responsive in coitus and eager to adopt children." I can assure you that she worked much harder than he did.

Being on bedrest gave me the time I needed to take this all in. For decades I was told I didn't have a uterus and then had two halves removed. I was blamed for the back injuries that were rooted in a congenital condition. I was rebuked for not paying attention when I simply couldn't hear. I was told I would never meet anyone like me, as the others like me had been told. Being surgically altered to satisfy a social concept confirmed why I feel erased and betrayed. It's been fifty years since my feminizing surgery and I still don't know who I am. Naming the lack of consent as systemic genocide helps to navigate that, but the reality still blows me away.

Holding Our Own

I looked down at my most recent stitches and cried. All that I knew about myself was now in question. MRKH was presented as a physical failure, resolved by the quick fix of medical correction that was neither quick nor correct. I had to unlearn EVERYTHING I had been taught to find my personal truth. I tried to be gentle with my emotions, hoping they would comfort me while I sorted all this out. I was wrong. Emotionally I was starting over as the person I was meant to be. The more I saw how I had been erased the harder that was to accept. There are no support systems for people who are invisible but systems are in place to keep us that way. Fortunately I was no longer alone.

The MRKH and Intersex communities were evolving in the 1990's, with the birth of social media. We were excited and awkward and traumatized. Meeting others was life altering and that momentum gave us hope. We became activists because we survived.

In 1999, I built a web site to share all the information I could find about MRKH and Intersex.* The following year I included my insider study in the first article about MRKH ever published from a personal perspective.* Activists performed it at V-Day events.* I was invited to speak at health conferences, LBGTQ conferences, medical schools and sociology classes. A friend helped me form a nonprofit in 2001 and I became an officer on two different boards.* A teen women's health center asked me to meet with their staff to discuss treatment protocols versus patient-centered care.*

Decades after those efforts began; Facebook, Instagram, YouTube and TicTok are on fire with gender expansive folks coming to terms with who they are. I envy them that community is available now. I remain grateful to the activists who pulled us from the dark.

My favorite line in the film INTERSEXION is, "But you're gonna have to change your mind now."* Initially I thought that meant that people have to accept the full spectrum of sex development and that is very true. That line grew with meaning as I drove through the woods to visit my best friend last summer. I realized I can also have hope for my future. I don't have to stay trapped by my past. I stopped the car and sat with this magical moment as the sunlight poured through the pines. By changing my mind, I now get to build the life for the MRKH/Intersex kid that no one wanted her to have. I didn't want to be the girl who could never measure-up, or a girl who needed surgery to become a real woman. I cannot honor who I am until I let go of who I am not.

Every time I tell my therapist, "I am a mess," she reminds me that I am not the mess but living in a messy world. She helped me respect my right to feel safe and to set boundaries around those who have none. My massage therapist, acupuncturist and chiropractor keep me engaged with my body. Qigong helps me channel psychic and physical pain. I reached a turning point when my primary care doctor questioned the muscle relaxants I had been taking for decades. I had to reconsider my approach to m body and I was scared. Really scared. I welcomed the vulnerability but I just couldn't shake the fear. Medication had masked the pain, and all that my pain represented. Nothing I endured, from work in the trades or physical rehab, compared to the healing I was taking on now. The damage to my discs was tangible but the somatic impact o sanctioned abuses was buried too deep to feel.

I started to work with a holistic physical therapist to address chronic pain without medication. My skin softened after the first visit. I could feel my breath grow deeper. The physical pain that restricted me for years was slowly easing. My body let go of tensions I didn't know I had been holding. I remembered dreams for the first time since childhood. Acknowledging my vulnerability felt powerful. Each area of pain that she worked on evoked ar emotional response. The tight knot in my left glute released the sad little girl who gave up that butt cheek for a vaginal skin graft. My rib cage relaxed, not needing to protect my heart as it had since my youth. My spirit connected with my body's wisdom; tapped into my grief and trauma then brought those feelings to light. I have grieved the loss of physical pride that being a tradeswoma gave me. I have grieved becoming a woman as defined by menstruation and fertility. When I started to grieve the child who was murdered by medicalization I found mysel sobbing for days. Deep, wrenching, guttural sobs that cam from a place inside me I had never felt before. I couldn't ignore my grief anymore; I simply had to be in it. I was shamed for being so different from other woman. Now that I know how truly expansive we are- normal can't shame me anymore.

Questions have haunted me for too many years because I couldn't find the words. Knowing others with similar experiences has helped me find my voice. Our diversity seems extreme only because it's unheard of. We exist in a conundrum because our knowledge is powerful but hidden in embarrassment and shame. The approach to our treatment might seem extreme but affects all women in subtler ways. Advances in medicine offer men Viagra, but women still get the knife. Scar tissue does not enhance sexual pleasure. Being born with "congenital absence of vagina" posed less of a threat to my health than the traits of MRKH that disabled me. But a skin graft vagina is all I was offered to cope with a much greater loss.

I'm still pretty mad that my culture celebrates diversity in every life form but our own. I have seen the response of too many twisted faces telling me they have never heard of people like me. They show me pity. They tell their friends this great gossip and strangers ask intrusive questions on the street corner. I have been assaulted by women who presumed I was Trans and too active in the women's community. I have been asked if this is what made me a lesbian, by lesbians who were born with vaginas.

Our diversity challenges the status quo and that makes people very nervous. We challenge the concepts of binary gender and normal sexual activity, which threatens others to their core. Variations of sex and gender exist in every culture, nationality, faith and race. We are your neighbors, your coworkers, your teachers, relatives, and your friends.

Some cultures regard their gender expansive people as Leaders, Elders, Two-spirit or Gifts from God. In our western medicalized culture, we have to go public with our privates to demand basic human rights. It's incredibly hard to do that, but it's harder to outlive the death of your soul.

As Massachusetts State Senator Ayanna Pressley said, "I look forward to the day when no one has to weaponize and relive their trauma to advance justice."*

And so do I, along with countless others.

* www.MRKH.org
* The Missing Vagina Monologue
* The MRKH Organization and the Intersex Society of North America.
* Center for Young Women's Health, Boston Children's Hospital
* Gavan Coleman's interview in the documentary, Intersexion intersexionfilm.com Available on Kanopy in some libraries. The 45 minute rough cut is on Amazon Prime.
* The Boston Day of Action, in Franklin Park, October 2, 2021

Epilogue

I am not as involved in the trades as I used to be but am told the culture is better for women and minorities now. In terms of physical autonomy, we seem to be going backwards. I started to understand something Robbie said all those years ago; that white supremacy hurts white people too. Nothing exercises privilege more than casting one's limited lens onto someone else's experience; then deciding what they need or how they should live their lives. Every day is full of systemic oppression from people in my own privileged, white communities. Our overwhelmingly white, male, heteronormative government makes decisions about lives they could never understand; restricting liberties and resources for that very reason. Our class system and social values are rooted in an elitist, white academic culture; full of titles and degrees, and biased values that determine language, learning styles, and success. Even the comparison used to quantify Intersex, "as common as red hair," conjures an image so white I can't cite it to the communities I spend time in. I was bowled-over when women in my faith community took control of an experience they didn't have and thought that made them allies. I resigned. And I have stumbled with my own privilege enough to know there are times when privilege should listen more and talk less.

As a person with inherited privilege, who has been tortured for the way I was born, I can't help but to see how the privilege I benefit from feeds the arrogance that caused my trauma. What I am learning from my own recovery not only helps me heal, but helps me see how I need to grow. We have to work on ourselves as much as we work to change our culture. It doesn't always serve to invite marginalized folks to the table. Until we know when to stand down, we have to give up our seats.

What You Should Know

1:2000 people are born with male or female sex / reproductive anatomy that does not conform to traditional standards. In most cases there is no threat to one's physical well-being.

There are dozens of conditions that fall under the Intersex umbrella.

95% of Genital surgeries are done for cosmetic reasons to reinforce the binary standard of normalcy.

Genital surgeries are nonreversible.

1:~1700 people have atypical chromosomes. The five most common chromosomes karyotypes are: XX, XY, XO, XXY, XYY. There are additional mosaic combinations that contribute to our diversity even more. We should update the definitions of "a man and a woman" rather than persecute the people who disprove them.

Most genital surgeries happen years before children, and their sex anatomy, have a chance to mature.

Pronouns are important so people can be recognized as the gender they identify with. They can also be traumatic

111

to those who are forced into binary norms without consent.

Success rates for genital surgeries are determined by medical outcomes, not patient satisfaction.

Nonconsensual genital surgeries are still the medical protocol.

In 2023, the number of US hospitals that have pledged a moratorium on nonconsensual genital surgeries on children in the United States can be counted on one hand

As of March 2023, there are more than 350 active Anti-Trans bills trying to control the way gender diverse folks live and present. At least two-thirds of those bills include ways to reinforce non-consensual genital surgery on kids with nonconforming anatomy. Restricting autonomy is the focus and autonomy impacts everyone.

The term, Disorders of Sex Development is used to label Intersex diversity as something that needs to be fixed.

Preventing emotional distress is often cited as the reason for nonconsensual genital surgeries. The surgical Intersex protocols developed by John Money were based on falsified data from a test case that failed. Each twin in that test case committed suicide as young adults. And yet the protocols remain...

Thank You Notes

- I have been blessed by an amazing village of healers. Thank you, thank you, thank you!

-Shout-out to tradeswomen; past, present and future!

- I am forever grateful to the early Intersex activists. Even though the trials of those early days were painful, I doubt we could have gotten here gently.

- Thank you to my mentor and friend, Pat Rieker for convincing me to use my voice.

- I am blessed to have people who make me feel safe not knowing where I belong. I can't list you all but the Leader of the Pack was my cousin Betty. Thank you for helping me learn how to trust and let humor soften my sadness...

- Shout-out to the SCOPE Crew and Voices of Liberation. You welcomed me as a proud Intersex person, and constantly show me intersectionality in practice.

- To my beloved family of choice, Ann and Jake: Your support, patience and love have been my comfort, even when it wasn't / isn't for you.

- To my MRKH and Intersex siblings: Your courage, advocacy and presence in my life are gifts that keep on giving. We started with nothing and have created our own communities. We will prevail!

- And thanks, Ma, for encouraging me to live my truth. And for making me write Thank You notes so I wouldn't take people for granted.

Things to Think About

1. Think about your gender identity without thinking about your anatomy. How would you feel if you were forbidden to feel that way? If you don't identify as one gender alone, how would you feel if you were forced to?

2. How do you feel when other people make decisions for your own good that are wrong? Now remember a time when you did that to someone else.

3. What are some experiences you might share with people you have nothing in common with culturally?

4. Do you believe everyone is entitled to the same basic human rights, even if equal rights challenge your social privilege or personal beliefs?

5. Have you ever had a physical response to an emotional experience, such as gasping when startled or jumping for joy? Consider the impact to your overall well-being if your sex anatomy were altered for the comfort of others.

Glossary

<u>Binary:</u> Either or. Binary gender is Male or Female. Nature offers so much more.
<u>Gender Expansive:</u> A term used to encourage us to see gender beyond the binary norms.
<u>Genderqueer:</u> umbrella term that includes those who don't identify with the traditional binary definitions of gender expression.
<u>Gender Identity:</u> How we feel about ourselves. Gender is not defined by our physical make up. Not all people with the same anatomy identify the same way. Identity is something that everyone should claim for themselves.
<u>Intersex:</u> An umbrella term for anyone born with sex or reproductive anatomy not defined as normal. Some people feel Intersex is a physical identity. Some people feel Intersex is a gender identity and other people use the term for both. Some people don't use this term at all.
<u>Medicalize:</u> To view people through a medical lens and not as individuals.
<u>MRKH:</u> Mayer-Rokitansky-Kuster-Hauser syndrome, also known as mullerian agenesis, involves congenital absence of vagina, uterus, cervix and fallopian tubes. Can also impact skeletal and hearing and renal development
<u>MRKH/INTERSEX:</u> a way to show that not all people with MRKH identify as Intersex, and there is more to Intersex than MRKH.

<u>Non-binary:</u> people who do not identify as male or female or may identify as both.

<u>Sex:</u> describes our physical make up as defined by our reproductive anatomy, genital anatomy and chromosomes. Male and female are extreme examples, but anatomy is far more diverse.

<u>Trans:</u> refers to people who do not identify to the sex or the gender they were assigned at birth. Although there may be some overlap, Trans and Intersex experiences are different.

Contact information
MRKH Organization
www.MRKH.org
MRKHorg@gmail.com
@NotUncommonEsther

References

Please note: many of these references are outdated, but sadly, still relevant. I've included them to show how far we've come and how far we still need to go.

Blackless, M., Anthony C., Amanda D., Fausto-Sterling A., Lauzanne, K. & Lee, E. (2000), How sexually dimorphic are we? Review and synthesis. American Journal of Human Biology, 12:151-166.

The Brussels Collaboration on Bodily Integrity, Medically Unnecessary Genital Cutting and the Rights of the Child: Moving Toward Consensus; The American Journal of Bioethics, 2019, VOL. 19, NO. 10, 17-28

Carmil, D., Bar-David, E., David, A. & Serr, D. M. (1975), Congenital absence of the vagina: clinical and physiologic aspects. Obstetrics and Gynecology, 46:407-409.

Ensler, E. (1998), The Vagina Monologues. New York: Villard Books.

Foley, S. & George W.M. (1992), Care and counseling of the patient with vaginal agenesis. The Female Patient, 17 October:73-80.

Kaplan, E.H. (1968), Congenital absence of vagina: Psychiatric aspects of diagnosis and management. New York State Journal of Medicine, 15:1937-1941.
Kutile, M.M. & Weijenborg, P. (2000), The effect of a group programme on women with the Mayer-Rokitansky-Kuster-Hauser syndrome. British Journal Obstetrics & Gynecology, 107:365-368.

Leidolf, Esther, published under the pseudonym Morris, Marguerite, The Missing Vagina Monologue, Sojourner, March 2001 [Vol 26, no7]. My deepest thanks to Rochelle Ruthchild and Amy Pett for their input and editing. Republished [Esther Morris Leidolf (2006) The Missing Vagina Monologue ... and Beyond, Journal of Gay & Lesbian Psychotherapy, 10:2, 77 92, DOI: 10.1300/J236v10n02_05] Available at www.mrkh.org

Lewis, V.G. & Money, J. (1986), Sexological theory, H-Y antigen, chromosomes, gonads, and cyclicity: Two syndromes compared. Arch. Sex. Behav., 15:467-474.

Money, J., Schwartz, M. & Lewis, V.G. (1984), Adult erotosexual status and fetal hormonal masculinization and demasculinization: 46,XX congenital virilizing adrenal hyperplasia and 46,XY androgen-insensitivity syndrome compared. Psychoneuroendocrinology, 9:405-414.

Raboch, J. & Horejsi, J. (1982), Sexual life of women with the Kuestner-Rokitansky syndrome. Arch. Sex. Behav., 11:215-220.

www.ingramcontent.com/pod-product-compliance
Lightning Source LLC
LaVergne TN
LVHW051248080426
835513LV00016B/1810